With love
from Nanna
Nov 24th 1953.

EAGLE BOOK OF
TRAINS

EAGLE BOOK OF TRAINS

by

CECIL J. ALLEN

Published by

HULTON PRESS LIMITED

London

First published 1953

Printed in Great Britain by Balding & Mansell Ltd., Wisbech

Contents

Colour Plates

Photograph Acknowledgements

Association of American Railroads, 26, 42, 43, 125 (*both*). Atchison, Topeka & Santa Fe Railroad, 25, 28, 77 (*lower*), 79, 155, 165. British Railways, 11, 14, 16, 17, 22, 24, 27 (*both*), 32, 45, 46, 47 (*both*), 48, 49 (*both*), 50, 58, 60, 67, 69 (*both*), 71 (*lower*), 72, 73, 74, 81 (*both*), 82 (*upper*), 94, 97, 100, 101 (*all*), 102, 103, 105 (*upper*), 106, 108, 109, 110, 118, 120 (*both*), 121, 122, 124, 132 (*both*), 133, 134, 135, 145 (*right upper*), 148, 149 (*all*), 150, 151 (*both*), 152, 174 (*both*), 180 (*both*), 182, 184, 188, 190. Burlington Lines, U.S.A., 116 (*upper*), 126 (*upper*), 127, 129, 130. Canadian National Railways, 20, 39, 54, 66, 68. Canadian Pacific Railway, 53, 61, 158, 175. Central Swiss Tourist Office, 172 (*both*). Chicago & North Western Railway, 145 (*lower*). Denver & Rio Grande Western Railroad, 19, 29, 144. M. W. Earley, 15 (*upper*), 44, 141. G. F. Fenino, 111. Furka-Oberalp Railway, 179. French National Railways, 35, 36 (*both*), 52. Great Northern Railway (Ireland), 77. Great Northern Railway (U.S.A.), 145 (*right upper*). Grisons Tourist Office, 163, 171, 175, 176. F. R. Hebron, 71 (*upper*). C. C. B. Herbert, 192. London Transport Executive, 75, 83, 84, 85 (*both*), 86 (*both*), 87, 88 (*both*), 89 (*both*), 90, 91, 92, 93, 161 (*both*). Lötschberg Railway, 30, 162. New South Wales Government Railways, 37, 38 (*lower*), 117. New York Central System, 115 (*both*), 138, 139. Norfolk & Western Railway, 113. Pennsylvania Railroad, 119, 126 (*lower*), 181. Picture Post Library, 10, 12, 13, 64 (*all*), 65 (*all*). Pilatus Railway, 170. Postmaster-General, 104 (*both*), 105 (*lower*). South African Railways, 21 (*upper*), 42, 55, 76, 137 (*both*), 142, 167. Southern Pacific Lines, 21 (*lower*), 114, 116 (*lower*), 164. Swiss Federal Railways, 33. Canon E. Treacy, 51, 62, 63, 140. Union Pacific Railroad, 82 (*lower*), 143, 147, 186, 187. Victorian Government Railways, 136. L. Vignier, 112, 156 (*lower*). Visp-Zermatt Railway, 178. Wengernalp & Jungfrau Railways, 169. E. R. Wethersett, 38 (*upper*).

Note : On page 9 'Locomotive No. 1' should read 'Locomotion No. 1'

CHAPTER I

How railways began

IT is curious to realize that the first railways were built long before there were any locomotives, and that the first locomotives in history did not run on railways but on the roads. In Central Europe, somewhere about 1550, the first primitive railways, with wooden rails, were laid down in the mines, for mine-owners found that it was much easier to push or pull wagons of minerals over a level and true track of this kind than over the ground. From about 1660 onwards, similar wagonways began to appear in the British coalfields, and in 1738 the first iron rails had been laid.

It was not until 1804 that the first railway in the world was opened for public traffic; it was known as the Surrey Iron Railway. Beginning by the side of the Thames at Wandsworth, it ran across Mitcham Common to Croydon, and was later extended to Merstham; you can still find traces of it at different points along the route. As yet there were no railway locomotives in general use; on the Surrey Iron Railway and all the other early railways and plateways the horse was still the motive power. But the possibility of using steam for traction in place of the horse was now stirring in men's minds, and the first steam locomotives had been invented and tried out, not on rails but on roads.

To Nicolas Cugnot, an obscure French mechanic, belongs the honour of having invented the first machine that ever moved itself by steam power. His curious 'steam carriage' may still be seen in a Paris Museum; it is believed to have got along the road at a speed of about three miles an hour! But at a demonstration in Paris in 1771 his invention unfortunately got out of hand, ran away, and overturned, injuring a number of spectators, so that poor Cugnot found himself in prison for his daring, rather than in popular favour.

At the same time a Scotsman named William Murdock, who was employed by the famous James Watt in supervising the erection of pumping engines at mines, was thinking along the same lines. In the quiet of the room in which he was living at Redruth, Murdock produced a model of a steam carriage. It is said that one dark night in 1786 when he was trying it out along the church path at Redruth, the vicar, seeing this strange apparition of smoke and flames, thought that he had met a demon in person, but this is probably a legend.

But a Cornish engineer named Trevithick, who lived at Redruth within a stone's throw of Murdock's lodgings, was the first inventor to connect in his mind the steam road carriage, on the one hand, and the primitive railways of his time, on the other. After some experiments with road carriages, at last Trevithick produced his first railway locomotive, and on 13th February 1804 it made its first public run, over the tramway which connected the Pen-y-Darran Ironworks with Merthyr Tydfil, in South Wales. All went well; the strange-looking

7

HOW IT ALL BEGAN

TRACKS TO TAKE VEHICLES USING A FIXED WHEEL GAUGE ARE EXTREMELY ANCIENT. MANY GREEK AND ROMAN TYPES CAN BE SEEN, BUT OLDER CIVILISATIONS ALMOST CERTAINLY POSSESSED THEM AS WELL.

BY THE 16TH CENTURY MINE RAILWAYS WITH WOODEN RAILS HAD BECOME QUITE COMMON IN CENTRAL EUROPE. THE RAILS WERE, OF COURSE, VERY ROUGHLY MADE, BUT WERE ADEQUATE FOR THEIR PURPOSE AS SHOWN IN THIS PICTURE, WHICH IS BASED ON AN OLD PRINT.

THE FIRST SERVICEABLE STATIONARY STEAM ENGINE WAS DESIGNED BY THOMAS NEWCOMEN IN 1712, BUT IT WAS THE FAMOUS JAMES WATT THAT FUNDAMENTALLY IMPROVED THE STATIONARY TYPE IN 1769. HERE IS ALL THAT REMAINS OF HIS "OLD BESS" ENGINE.

IN THE 17TH CENTURY BRITAIN TOOK THE LEAD IN COAL MINING AND DEVELOPED WAGON WAYS ON A BIG SCALE. THE FIRST GREAT RAILWAY BRIDGE WAS BUILT IN 1726 — THE TANFIELD ARCH (103 FEET WIDE). IT STILL STANDS AND ORIGINALLY CARRIED A DOUBLE TIMBER TRACK OF 4 FT. GAUGE.

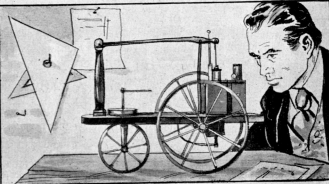

ALTHOUGH THE FRENCHMAN, CUGNOT, MADE THE FIRST MOVING STEAM CARRIAGE (IN 1769) IT WAS THE CORNISHMAN, WILLIAM MURDOCK, WHO (IN 1786) GAVE THE IDEA A REAL START. HERE HE IS EXAMINING HIS MODEL WHICH IS REPUTED TO HAVE UNNERVED THE LOCAL VICAR.

THE TWIN STORIES OF WAGON TRACK AND STEAM ENGINE

STEAM CARRIAGES PROGRESSED UNTIL IN THE 1830'S THEY BECAME EXTRAORDINARY AFFAIRS LIKE THIS VERSION OF THE OLD STAGE COACH. THEY NATURALLY ENCOUNTERED OPPOSITION, BUT ALTHOUGH REGARDED AS DANGEROUS THEY FORTUNATELY DID NOT REQUIRE ANYTHING MORE THAN A PASSABLY GOOD ROAD.

MEANWHILE, HOWEVER, ANOTHER CORNISHMAN — RICHARD TREVITHICK — WAS WORKING ON THE STEAM CARRIAGE IDEA AND IN 1804 PROVED IT WAS POSSIBLE TO RUN ONE ON RAILS AND SO INVENTED THE FIRST AUTHENTIC RAIL-WAY LOCOMOTIVE.

HERE IS THE SCENE IN LONDON WHEN IT WAS BEING DEMONSTRATED IN 1808 NEAR EUSTON

THE GREATEST NAME IN EARLY RAILWAYS IS THAT OF GEORGE STEPHENSON, WHO NOT ONLY DESIGNED LOCOMOTIVES FROM 1814 ONWARDS BUT THE TRACKS AND ROLLING STOCK. IN 1825 HE DROVE HIS OWN ENGINE "LOCOMOTIVE Nº 1" AT THE OPENING OF THE FIRST PUBLIC STEAM RAILWAY. IT HAULED SOME 90 TONS OF WAGONS AND THEIR CONTENTS, WAS PRECEDED BY A MAN WITH A RED FLAG AND MOVED AT A LITTLE OVER 10 MILES PER HOUR.

FINALLY CAME HIS CROWNING SUCCESS IN 1829 WITH HIS "ROCKET" WINNING THE RAINHILL TRIALS AGAINST ALL COMPETITORS. THE TASK WAS TO DRAW A LOAD OF 20 TONS AT 10 MILES PER HOUR, AND THE "ROCKET" NOT ONLY IMPROVED CONSIDERABLY ON THAT, BUT RAN AT A SPEED OF ABOUT 30 MILES PER HOUR WHEN LIGHTLY LOADED.

The original *Puffing Billy*, **which first fired the imagination of the young George Stephenson as it ran noisily over the Wylam Tramway. The vertical cylinders, one on each side of the boiler, drove up and down the horizontal beams above the boiler, which were connected by vertical rods to the cranks between the wheels; these turned a shaft which was geared to the driving axles.** *Puffing Billy* **began to run in 1813.**

machine pulled a load of 25 tons on level track, and reached a speed of five miles an hour

A London engineer who watched the trial was tremendously impressed. So much so, indeed, that in writing an account of what he had seen, he claimed that the new 'wagon engine', as he called it, would be able to pump water out of the mines, then wind the coal up to the surface, pull the coal along the track, and between whiles it would be able to work a steam hammer!

Twenty-one years later there came the opening of the first railway in the world on which public traffic was to be worked by steam power. It was the Stockton & Darlington Railway, in the County of Durham, and it introduces us to the most famous of all railway pioneers, George Stephenson. He was the son of an agricultural labourer on Tyneside, who earned no more than twelve shillings a week on which to keep himself and his wife and six children; so George had no advantages of education. But the cottage in which he lived, at Wylam-on-Tyne, stood beside the Wylam Colliery line, on which he would see *Puffing Billy* and some of the other early locomotives, laboriously drawing their trains of coal, and this fired his imagination. Eventually he became engine-wright at the Killingworth High Pit, and it was there that he designed and built his first engine, the *Blucher*.

Soon he came under the notice of Edward Pease, a prominent man in Darlington, who had the idea of laying a railway from the coal mines to the north-west of Darlington to the River Tees at Stockton; and in 1822 he appointed Stephenson, now 41 years old, to be the Engineer of his line. So it was that when the opening day came, on 27th September 1825, it was Stephenson who had engineered and laid the line, who had designed and built its wagons and the locomotive — *Locomotion No. 1*, which is still preserved on a pedestal at the Bank Top Station in Darlington — and who was actually driving the engine on this historic occasion. Although only 6½ tons in weight, *Locomotion No. 1* is credited with a top speed of 12 miles an hour.

It is striking to recall that one hundred and ten years later, to the very day, on the inaugural run of the London & North Eastern Railway 'Silver Jubilee' streamliner — which would stop at Darlington daily from then onwards — exactly one hundred miles an hour was added to the speed of *Locomotion No. 1*, for the new Pacific locomotive *Silver Link* twice touched 112½, and reeled off 43 miles continuously at an average of exactly 100 miles an hour.

Four years after the opening of the Stockton & Darlington Railway, Stephenson produced his famous *Rocket*. The first railway connecting two British cities — the Liverpool & Manchester — was about to be opened, and the Directors had offered a prize of £500 to the inventor who could produce the most reliable locomotive for working their trains. Trials were held at a place called Rainhill, near Liverpool; each competitor must be able to draw a load of 20 tons at ten miles an hour, must not weigh more than 6 tons, nor require a steam pressure higher than 50 pounds to the square inch.

George Stephenson's *Locomotion No. 1*, designed and built by him for the opening of the first public railway in the world, from Stockton-on-Tees to Darlington, and driven by Stephenson on the opening day, 27th September 1825. It weighed 6½ tons, and the tender 2¼ tons, cost £600, and is credited with speeds up to 12 m.p.h. It is still preserved on a pedestal in Bank Top Station, Darlington.

Stephenson's famous *Rocket*, which won the prize of £500 offered by the Directors of the Liverpool & Manchester Railway at the Rainhill contest of 1829. Each competitor had to run 35 miles, twice in succession, at an average of not less than 10 m.p.h., representing a journey from Liverpool to Manchester and back. The *Rocket* completed its tests at an average of 19 m.p.h. and reached a maximum speed of 29 m.p.h. This is a model of the historic engine.

Of the four competitors, the *Rocket* was an easy winner; it did considerably better than what was required by covering 35 miles with the test train in 1 hour 50 minutes, and when running light it got up to 29 miles an hour. With the opening of the Liverpool & Manchester Railway in 1830, railway transport was now firmly on its feet. But the people who were anxious to see railway communication established did not have an easy time at first. Every new project had to be sanctioned by Act of Parliament, and those who opposed the coming of railways, for various reasons, prophesied that terrible results would follow the running of steam engines through the countryside. Cattle would be terrified and horses rendered unmanageable; birds would be suffocated and vegetation destroyed; children would be frightened and the whole countryside devastated.

But with the opening of some of the more important lines, such as that from Euston terminus in London to Birmingham in stages from 1837 to 1838, and from Paddington to Bristol from 1838 to 1841, a progress had begun that nothing could stop. By the year 1846, railways had taken such a hold on the popular imagination that no fewer than 1,263 Bills were presented to Parliament seeking authority to build new railways, and though no more than 272 of these became law, railway building by now was proceeding very fast indeed.

Some of the memories of this period are very amusing. When the London & Birmingham Railway was opened, the management was approached to know if they would be prepared to carry coal over their line. One of the Directors held up his hands in horror. 'What?' he said, 'Coal? Why, we shall be expected to carry dung next!' And when eventually it was agreed that this obnoxious mineral should be allowed to travel over the railway, a high screen was erected between the railway line and the Grand Junction Canal at Weedon, where the coal was transferred from the railway trucks to canal barges, so that no passengers in the trains should see this vulgar transaction in progress! Today the railways would find it very difficult to make ends meet without their coal traffic, which forms the backbone of railway revenue, and is considerably more profitable than the carriage of passengers.

A few more dates are worth recalling. The first railway to pay special attention to the safe working of its trains was the Great Western, which installed Cook & Wheatstone's electric telegraph between Paddington and West Drayton in 1838. This contribution to safety was brought prominently under notice in 1846, when Queen Victoria decided to make her first journey by train, from Slough to Paddington. A tremendous step forward was taken in 1872, when both the Midland and Great Eastern Railways decided that third-class passengers should be allowed to travel by all their trains; until then, the best and fastest trains were all either first and second-class only, or in some cases were limited to first-class passengers alone.

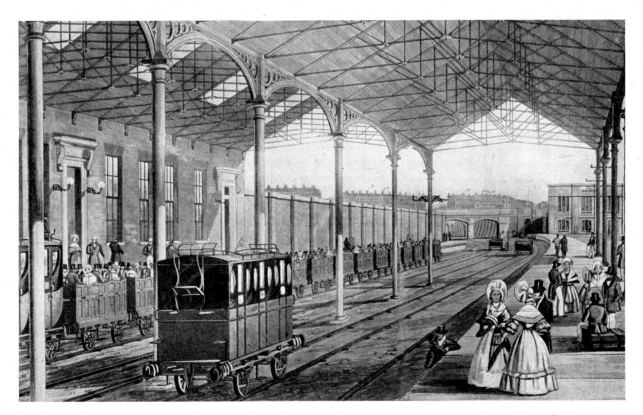

Euston Station, London, at the time of the opening of the London & Birmingham Railway in 1837. Third-class passengers rode in open wagons and only second- and first-class passengers were provided with seats in covered compartments. The guard had to ride at roof level on the seat seen at the end of the coach in the foreground. Some of the original Euston still remains as part of the present station.

Half-a-century of locomotive development. On the left is No. 1 of the old Great Northern Railway, a Stirling 8 ft. single-wheeler, and on the right a streamlined Pacific of the London & North Eastern Railway, No. 4498 *Sir Nigel Gresley.* **The photograph was taken in 1938.**

By 1859 the first sleeping car had been introduced by an American named Pullman — who later was to achieve world-wide fame with his luxury coaches — and in 1867 the first dining car appeared in Canada; but it took some time for these ideas to get across the Atlantic to Great Britain. At last, in 1873, first-class sleeping cars started to run between King's Cross, London, and Edinburgh; then, in the following year, the Midland Railway brought into use some Pullman cars; and the first British dining car took its place on the Great Northern Railway between King's Cross and Leeds in 1879. Passengers in the early dining cars had to ride in them throughout the journey; it was not until 1892 that the first British train took the rails with a passage through it from end to end, so that passengers could reach a dining car from another part of the train. This was on the Great Western Railway.

In 1883 there was a railway opening which marked a milestone in railway history. It was no more than a six-mile tramway, from Portrush to Bushmills, in Northern Ireland, but for the first time, a little uncertainly, perhaps, the passengers in its cars were moved, not by steam, but by electricity. Seven years later, in 1890, there came the opening of the City & South London Railway, which was not only the first electrically-worked underground railway in the world, but also the first section of the great London tube system.

Today, practically the whole of the railways of Switzerland are worked by electricity, and a very large proportion of those in Sweden, France, Austria, and other countries, where steam locomotives have been largely displaced. It is interesting to note that electrified railways on the mainland of Europe depend principally for their current on the power of the water that rushes down from the higher levels in mountainous countries, just as the current for the primitive electric tramway at Portrush was generated from a local stream.

14

On Brunel's original main line to the west — a Paddington-Bristol express of the Great Western Railway leaving Box Tunnel, just over $1\frac{3}{4}$ miles long. When opened, in 1841, the Box Tunnel accommodated two broad gauge tracks, of 7 ft. gauge; conversion to the standard 4 ft. $8\frac{1}{2}$ in. gauge took place in 1892.

Opened in 1850, the Britannia Tubular Bridge, across the Menai Straits between North Wales and the island of Anglesey, was the greatest of all Robert Stephenson's engineering achievements. Each of the two rectangular tubes which carry the trains is 1,510 ft. long and weighs 4,680 tons.

Saltash Bridge, by which Brunel carried the Penzance main line of the Great Western Railway across the Tamar from Devon into Cornwall. The bridge floor is suspended from the 17 ft. diameter hollow elliptical curved tubes that form the upper part of the structure; each main span is 455 ft. across. Foundations for the centre pier were sunk 80 ft. below the water level. The bridge was opened in 1859.

Another development in motive power has been of much later date. Somewhere about the year 1925, the first experiments were made in the use of diesel power for driving trains. By the early 1930's the Germans had introduced their first diesel-electric streamline trains, with diesel engines driving generators, which in their turn produced the current for driving the train motors. With these German streamliners there came in speeds up to 100 miles an hour as a regular daily practice. The idea went across the Atlantic to the United States, where it has spread like a prairie fire.

By the end of 1952, American railways between them had over 20,000 diesel-electric loco-motive units in service which had taken over three-quarters of all the passenger trains and shunting work, and two-thirds of all the freight haulage. Thousands on thousands of steam locomotives have been thrown out of work and scrapped; in course of time steam seems likely to disappear as completely from the United States as it has done already from Switzerland. And now a new competitor has come on the scene in the shape of the gas-turbine-electric locomotive. So revolutionary changes are taking place on the railways today.

It only remains to chronicle two other historic happenings that have had a tremendous influence on the railways of Great Britain. The First World War affected the working of the railways so profoundly that, after it was over, the decision was reached by Parliament to group all the railways together, so that the more prosperous and wealthy companies might come to the help of some others which would find it difficult to carry on in the new conditions.

16

So an Act was passed in 1921, and came into force at the beginning of 1923, whereby all British railways were brought into four large groups.

The Great Western Railway remained more or less unaltered; the London & North Western, Midland, Caledonian, Glasgow & South Western, and Highland Railways became the London Midland & Scottish; the Great Northern, Great Central, Great Eastern, North Eastern, North British, and Great North of Scotland became the London & North Eastern; and the London & South Western, South Eastern & Chatham, and London, Brighton & South Coast became the Southern. With the old historic names there disappeared much that had made British railways so interesting, especially all the different designs and colours of locomotives and coaches. But the new arrangement was not destined to continue for more than a quarter of a century, at the end of which there came the Second World War. After this it was decided that the time had come for the nation to take over the country's railways, and from 1st January 1948, therefore, British Railways came into being. While it will be a long time, of course, before all traces of the individual railways have disappeared, more and more shall we see locomotives, carriages and wagons of the same standard designs taking over the working of the country's railways, and, almost inevitably, with the disappearance of the variety, there is bound to be some diminution of the interest. So we are fortunate to be alive while much of the old and varied railway interest still remains.

Tring Cutting, on the main line of the London Midland Region, British Railways, from Euston to the North. It formed a part of the original London & Birmingham Railway, and its 60 ft. depth was excavated entirely by hand, for no modern earth-moving machinery was in use at that early date. The navvies, with the barrows of soil that they had cut out with their spades, were pulled up the steep cutting sides by ropes.

B

CHAPTER 2

The railway engineer at work

IT is a very costly business to build a railway. In their early days, railways had the field to themselves, and up to the end of the nineteenth century they had spread all over the world to a total distance of nearly 700,000 miles. But the coming of the internal combustion engine has altered everything. Millions of motor vehicles have been built, and the roads have been improved to such an extent to carry them that the building of new railways is no longer a paying proposition; the aeroplane, which requires only its landing grounds and no tracks on which to run, is another formidable competitor. As a result, it is only in undeveloped countries that we are likely to see new railways of any length built in the future; on the other hand, the closing of branches and minor lines that pay no longer is going on much faster than new construction.

There are many reasons why railway building is so expensive. In view of the weight of modern locomotives and rolling stock, and the speed at which the trains travel, the track and the bridges must be very substantial. If high speed is intended, sharp curves must be avoided, and the gradients must be kept at a moderate figure. While the straight and level line may be easy to lay out in flat country, like the prairies of North America, it is a different matter when railways have to be carried through the mountains.

Over its old main line from Paddington to Taunton the Western Region of British Railways has scarcely a gradient worth mention for over 160 miles; across the Nullarbor Desert in the heart of Australia the East-West Transcontinental line is dead straight for 328 miles, the greatest length of railway in the world without a curve. But in hilly and mountainous country, railways sometimes run for mile after mile without a single stretch of straight or level track, unless it be through tunnels.

The heavier and faster the traffic that is intended over any new route, so much the more must the engineer try to keep down the steepness of the gradients and the sharpness of the curves, and his building costs are likely to go up in proportion. For really fast running, a main line should be laid with gradients not steeper than, say, 1 in 200 — that is, a total rise of 1 foot for every 200 feet travelled in a forward direction. But this is often impossible in the mountains; the London Midland main line of British Railways, for example, has to climb four miles at 1 in 75 to Shap Summit in order to make its way through the Westmorland fells, and there are ten miles right off at much the same figure to get the continuation of the same line over Beattock Summit in the Scottish Lowlands.

But what is that to the 18 miles mostly at 1 in 40 that carry the Gotthard main line in Switzerland up the valley of the Reuss to the great Gotthard tunnel? Or the far worse 1 in 28½

In the Royal Gorge, Colorado — an express of the Denver & Rio Grande Western R.R. winds its way along the bank of the Arkansas River. The road suspension bridge seen in the background is 1,050 ft. above the river bed.

that faces a westbound train of the Atchison, Topeka & Santa Fe Railroad in the U.S.A. before it can complete its climb to the 7,622-feet Raton Summit in New Mexico, on the way from Chicago and Kansas City to Los Angeles? Tremendously steep gradients like these increase out of all proportion the cost of working the trains, because of the higher power output needed, which may call for two or three or even more locomotives to each train.

Railway routes in large measure follow the river valleys; in the mountains the engineer has no option, apart from tunnelling, which he will avoid as far as possible, because tunnels in general are the most costly form of railway construction. Often in his planning he will deliberately make the line longer in order to ease the gradients. He may do this by turning from the main valley up which he is carrying his line into a lateral valley, climbing steadily up the latter and doubling back on the opposite side in a great loop, finally emerging in the main valley at a far greater altitude than that at which he left it.

Another favourite dodge to gain height in a narrow mountain valley is the spiral tunnel. As you climb the Reuss Valley on the Gotthard main line of the Swiss Federal Railways, for example, you come to a point beyond Gurtnellen at which the line suddenly turns into the mountain wall on the west side of the valley. You may not realize, in the train, that you are being carried, in the darkness, round a complete corkscrew turn in the rock, but there is no mistake about it when you emerge and see, 115 feet below you on the mountainside, the track over which you were travelling only a few moments previously.

A few miles further on, abreast of the village of Wassen, the railway first dives into the mountain wall on the east side of the valley, in which it makes a half corkscrew turn to reverse its direction, then proceeds backwards through the village, climbing all the time, and finally

19

The two great main lines across the width of Canada — the Canadian Pacific and the Canadian National — use the same river valleys for the last 400 miles into Vancouver. They are seen here on the opposite banks of the Fraser River, British Columbia.

passes through a third semi-spiral tunnel in order to regain its original southward direction, having thus made a double loop in the shape of a great 'S'. In this way over four miles are added to the distance, but the gradient is kept down to a maximum steepness of 1 in $38\frac{1}{2}$; actually the line is lifted roughly 400 feet in altitude in this way as it passes Wassen.

The greatest art of the railway engineer is seen in the way in which he uses every possible natural foothold in order to keep down his costs of construction. This means a most careful study of contours, for if he can carry his line round the contours without too sharp curvature, he avoids a great deal of unnecessary excavation of cuttings and tipping of embankments. In the mountains this is all the more important, because cuttings inevitably mean a great deal of blasting of rock to make a foothold for the track.

In a country like England, however, cuttings in general have been through soil rather than rock, and were new railways to be made here in modern conditions, it would be possible for the engineer to call to his aid all kinds of modern earth-moving machinery. These would make the task quite simple as compared, say, with the herculean human labour of excavating great cuttings like those at Tring and Roade, in preparation for the opening of the London & Birmingham Railway in 1837.

One minor point that might not occur to you is that the engineer, in planning his railway, has to make his earthworks 'balance' as nearly as he can. That is to say, the material he excavates for his cuttings should roughly equal what he requires to make his embankments. Otherwise it will be necessary to buy extra land, either to find a dumping ground for the surplus spoil from the cuttings, or from which to cut out enough soil to finish the banks. The

Maximum development on a narrow gauge. The 'Orange Express' leaves Capetown on its 1,300-mile journey to Kimberley, Bloemfontein, Ladysmith, Pietermaritzburg and Durban, entirely over a gauge 3 ft. 6 in. wide. The 4–8–2 locomotive is bigger than the biggest British Pacific locomotive, and the coaches are as wide as those in Britain.

The 'Overland' main line of the Southern Pacific R.R., from Ogden to San Francisco, crosses the 31½-mile width of the Great Salt Lake, Utah, by 12 miles of trestle viaduct and 19½ miles of rock causeway dumped on to the lake bed. The train is the streamliner 'City of San Francisco', on its way from Chicago to Oakland Pier, San Francisco.

A part of the complicated junctions at Camden, London Midland Region. By a system of tunnels, the approach to one of which is seen in the centre foreground, electric trains from both Euston and Broad Street burrow across to the electric line tunnels (which are out of sight to the right of the main Primrose Hill tunnel entrances in the background) without fouling any of the steam tracks.

route may even be varied, if this can be done without too much curvature, in order to secure the best results.

After the embankment has reached a certain height, it becomes more economical to build a viaduct; a viaduct is essential, of course, if a stretch of water is to be crossed, or a valley liable to flooding. In the same way, recourse will be had to tunnelling rather than to excavating a very deep cutting, though, as we have seen already, tunnelling will be avoided if possible. Tunnels are most frequent in mountain country, such as the spiral tunnels of which we have thought, or tunnels through projecting spurs in the valleys, or the great tunnels under the crests of mountain ranges that lead from one valley to another. But the world's biggest railway tunnels and bridges have the next chapter to themselves, so we need not deal with them here.

When at last the engineer has completed the path for the trains, or the 'formation', as it is called, there comes the important business of laying the track. First of all, a solid foundation of broken stone is laid; then, above that, the ballast, usually of crushed granite or similar stone. This has to form a firm basis for the sleepers, and to provide for drainage, so that water drains away rapidly from the track after heavy rainfall; the ballast also holds the sleepers securely in position. The sleepers themselves tie the rails together at exactly the right distance apart — the 'gauge', as it is called — and help to distribute the weight of the trains over the

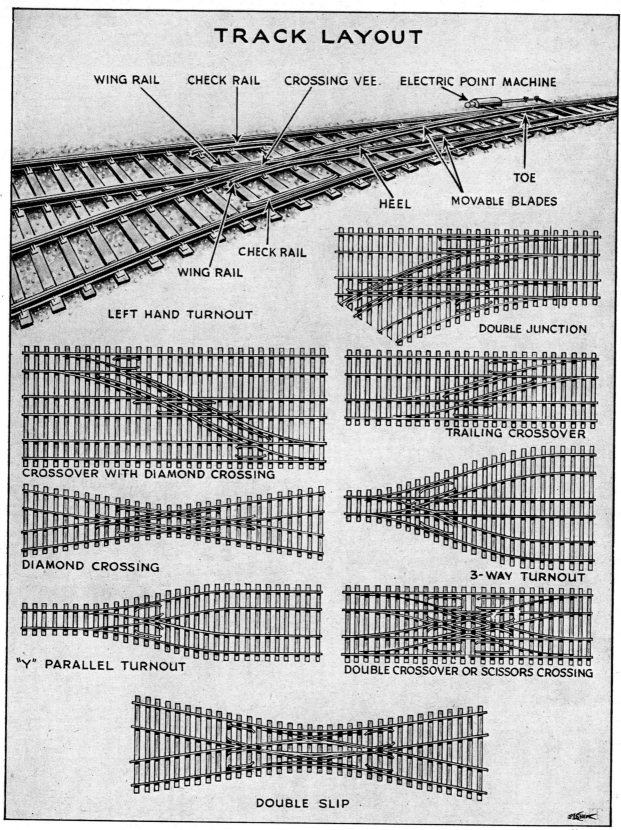

TRACK LAYOUT

WING RAIL   CHECK RAIL   CROSSING VEE   ELECTRIC POINT MACHINE

TOE

HEEL   MOVABLE BLADES

CHECK RAIL

WING RAIL

LEFT HAND TURNOUT

DOUBLE JUNCTION

CROSSOVER WITH DIAMOND CROSSING

TRAILING CROSSOVER

DIAMOND CROSSING

3-WAY TURNOUT

"Y" PARALLEL TURNOUT

DOUBLE CROSSOVER OR SCISSORS CROSSING

DOUBLE SLIP

A junction laid with modern flat-bottom rails. A track with the older bull-head rail, secured in chairs with keys, is on the left.

ballast. One has only to listen to an express thundering over the track at high speed to realize how vital it is that all the track shall be kept in first-class order, properly supported and firmly held in place.

No doubt you have noticed that in recent years, in Great Britain, a new type of steel rail has come into use. In the past we were always accustomed to what is called the 'bull-head' rail, in cross-section rather like a dumbbell, wedged into position in a series of cast iron 'chairs' by means of wooden or steel 'keys'. We have been familiar with the sight of the 'platelayers', with their hammers, walking along the track and driving the keys, or replacing those that have worked out. The new rail, however, has a flat foot, and although a cast iron baseplate is inserted between the rail and the sleepers, so that the steel shall not cut into the timber, no keys are needed to keep the rail securely in place. Instead, the foot of the rail is held down at each sleeper by three little curved spikes made of spring steel. Why has this change been made?

Actually, Great Britain has been practically the only country in the world to continue the use of the 'bull-head' rail; in almost every other country the 'flat-bottom' rail has been and still is standard. The advantage of the latter is that it is stiffer; it is deeper than the bull-head rail and has its wide foot, so that it cannot bend so easily. As a result, when once the flat-bottom rail has been properly laid, it keeps in line better, and needs less attention.

The rails used in Great Britain are 60 feet in length, and weigh 109 pounds to the yard. But they are quite light in comparison with some of the biggest rails used in the United States, where engines and trains are so heavy that the Pennsylvania Railroad, for one, lays a rail weighing no less than 155 pounds to the yard. However, in Great Britain, in general, we use much longer rails that the Americans; indeed, before the war the London & North Eastern and London Midland & Scottish Railways had some rails rolled which were no less than 120 feet in length.

There is a great advantage in laying rails as long as reasonably possible, because the longer the rails, so the joints between the rails become fewer and fewer. Not only are the rail-joints responsible for the characteristic 'clickety-click — clickety-click' that you hear all the time

On the footplate

This footplate drawing of a Class '7' Pacific locomotive of British Railways shows a typical cab layout for all the new standard locomotive classes. The cab is planned in such a way that the driver, from his seated position, has all his controls within reach, and so can maintain an uninterrupted lookout ahead. The fittings with which the fireman is chiefly concerned are grouped equally conveniently on his side of the cab. Instead of the usual hinged flap forming the continuation of the footplate between engine and tender, in the standard engines the engine footplate itself is extended to the tender front, so that the fireman can move between the tender front and the firehole door on a firm, flat platform.

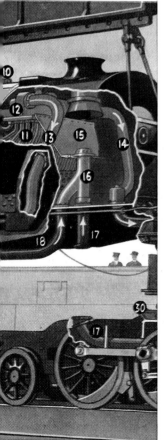

An articulated locomotive

Articulation is designed to spread the weight of a powerful locomotive over a considerable length of track, but at the same time the wheelbase must be flexible enough to traverse the curves in the track. This Beyer-Garratt example, in use on the South African Railways, consists of two independent 4–8–2 chassis, each with its own cylinders and motion, and each carrying, through the medium of a massive pivot, one end of the heavy girder frame that supports the boiler. The one boiler supplies steam to both ends of the engine, and is manned, of course, by one crew. Because each chassis is pivoted, and can adjust itself to the curves independently of the other, the limitation on curve negotiation is not that of the total 81 feet wheelbase of the locomotive, but of the single chassis wheelbase of 13 feet, $4\frac{1}{2}$ inches only. This remarkable 4–8–2–2–8–4 locomotive has been built for a track gauge no more that 3 feet 6 inches in width.

(FOR COLOUR PLATES OF ABOVE SEE OVER)

BRITISH R

KEY TO
'GARRATT' LOCO

(1) Firehole door. (2) B
(3) Inner firebox. (4) Fire
(5) Safety-valves. (6) Boi
tion. (7) Superheater flues
tubes. (8) Steam dome, with
valve under. (9) Main st
(10) Top feed, by which
introduced into boiler. (
heater tubes. (12) Superhea
(13) Main steam-pipe fr
heater to rear unit. (14) S
to front unit. (15) Spar
(16) Blast-pipe. (17) Exh
from front unit. (18) Ex
from rear unit. (19) Fle
nections for steam and
pipes, front unit. (20) Piv
unit. (21) Steam-operated
gear. (22) Water injector
(23) Ashpan below firebox.
of rear unit. (25) Rear piv
and flexible connections
and exhaust pipes. (26) 1
bunker. (27) Water filling
strainer. (28) Rear water
gallons capacity. (29) Vac
cylinder. (30) Front pivot s
flexible connections. (31)
coupled wheels. (32) W
valve-motion. (33) Piston-
Piston. (35) Buckeye
coupling. (36) Vacuum b
connection. (37) Electric
(38) Front water tank, 3,3
capacity. (39) Water filling
strainer. (40) Air vent to v

A Santa Fe train of the type used in the United States to detect internal defects in rails. The cars travel slowly along the track, passing an electric current between two brushes along the rail-head; any interruption of the flow by a defect causes a pen to mark a moving paper roll in the observer's compartment. By discovering and removing faulty rails, accidents due to broken rails are avoided.

you are travelling in the train, but they are the weakest part of the track as well, and need much the most attention. So nowadays a great deal is being done to reduce the number of joints by welding the rails together in long continuous lengths.

Now everyone who hears this immediately asks, 'But what about expansion? Don't you leave a space between each pair of rails to allow them to expand in hot weather?' The answer is simple. Although steel wants very badly to expand as the temperature rises, it can be prevented from doing so if you hold it tightly enough. Thus, if the rails are very tightly secured in place throughout their length, they will not move, even in the hottest weather; the urge to expand is always there, but it is not allowed to act. As the temperature drops again, so the urge is lost, and the steel returns to its normal condition internally.

In Great Britain a lot of continuous rail welding has been done in the tube tunnels under London, and this, with certain other measures that have been taken to reduce noise, explains why, during recent years, travelling on many of the London tubes has become so much quieter

Inside the rail detector car. The moving paper roll on which rail defects appear is under the observer's hand. When a defect is discovered, a splash of paint or whitewash is dropped on the affected rail, to identify it.

than before. On the surface railways, many welded rails from 180 to 300 feet long have been laid down.

But this is nothing to what has happened on an American railway called the Elgin, Joliet & Eastern, which carries freight traffic round the southern outskirts of the city of Chicago. This company has been steadily welding rails into 1,600-feet lengths, carrying them on a string of wagons to the place where they are to be laid in, and then welding the 1,600-feet lengths into vastly longer lengths as they lie in the track. The Elgin, Joliet & Eastern now has one continuous rail no less than 19,812 feet long, or more than *three miles and a half!* It is with little doubt the longest steel rail in the world.

The railway track is known as the 'permanent way', although actually it is anything but permanent. Rails wear away under the action of the millions of wheels that roll over them; sleepers decay or split; ballast gradually gets dirty, so that the drainage system begins to suffer. In some tropical countries wooden sleepers would get eaten up completely by white ants, and steel sleepers must be used instead. In all countries that use wooden sleepers, they have to be made to absorb large quantities of creosote oil or mineral salts, so that they may be protected as far as possible from the tendency to rot. Concrete sleepers might be used more than they are, were it not that they tend to crack in use, and are so cumbersome to handle. There is nothing like timber, if enough of it can be obtained.

Because the track is not permanent, from time to time it must be renewed. When the work is about to begin, up go the warning signs at the side of the track — a yellow warning board half-a-mile away, to tell the drivers of oncoming trains to slow down, then a 'C' sign to show exactly where the work begins, and a 'T' sign at the far end, to show the termination of the work, from which normal speed may be resumed. In old days, after the dirty ballast had been shovelled out, the work of 'relaying' went on, in the intervals between the passing trains, bit by bit until it was finished, but nowadays there are much quicker methods.

Entire sixty-feet lengths of track, rails, chairs, sleepers and all, are assembled at central depots, and loaded on long wagons. On a Saturday night, after the normal rush of traffic is ended, the Engineer's staff obtain complete possession of the track that is being relaid, no trains being allowed to pass over it until the work is finished. A string of the wagons loaded with lengths of track is then run to the site, together with powerful cranes of a special design, which lift the old track out, length by length, and drop in the new. Meantime, single line working is in force, and all trains in both directions use the other track only.

During the Sunday, perhaps a whole mile of new track goes into position; the rails are joined together by their 'fishplates', and 'lined up', and by Sunday evening the train service over the length of affected track

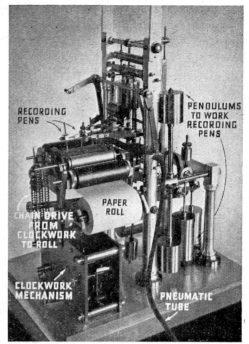

The Hallade Recorder, which when carried in a train draws a diagram of the oscillations on a moving paper roll, so locating track irregularities.

On Sundays in the spring, engineers take complete possession of the Severn Tunnel for repair work and track relaying. The old track, in 60 ft. lengths, is lifted out bodily, and the new track, in pre–assembled lengths, is laid in, by the special track-laying train shown.

may be resumed. Trains still have to run slowly for a time, while the ballast is carefully packed under the sleepers until a surface as nearly perfect as possible has been obtained, and then full speed running once again becomes possible.

How is the surface of a railway track checked to ensure that it is in the best possible running order? An instrument called a 'Hallade Recorder', of French origin, is carried in a compartment of an express train. On a moving paper roll, driven by clockwork, a number of pens, actuated by a system of pendulums, record every movement of the coach, including side lurches, or bumps up and down, or anything else that may indicate that the track needs attention.

Sometimes these recorders are carried in a special car attached to the back of the train, which drops a splash of whitewash on to the track at the exact point where some unusual movement has been recorded. This length of track is then given special attention by the maintenance gang responsible. In this way a close watch can be kept on the track, and the smooth and safe riding which is the proud boast of the railway engineer can be ensured.

A very important part of track maintenance is 'tamping', or keeping the sleepers well packed up on the ballast. Here, on the Santa Fe R.R., it is being done by a mechanical tamper, which saves much manual labour. It can be lifted off the track when a train is signalled.

CHAPTER 3

The world's biggest bridges and tunnels

I
N the mind of the railway engineer the word 'impossible' does not exist. To find proof that this assertion is true we have only to look around the world and see some of the amazing feats that engineers have carried out in order to make a path for the trains. Nature puts many formidable obstacles in the engineer's way, and it is a study of great interest to find how these obstacles have been penetrated, or crossed, or at times circumvented by means of a more circuitous course. It is in carrying railways through mountain ranges, needless to say, that the greatest tasks of tunnelling have been achieved; but in the very nature of things these cannot be so spectacular to the onlooker as bridges by which deep valleys, and, above all, wide water-ways, have been spanned.

It is a curious fact that the longest continuous tunnel in the world is found underneath

Moffat Tunnel, 6¼ miles, second longest in the United States, and 9,200 ft. above sea level. No part of the 570-mile main line of the Denver & Rio Grande Western R.R., from Denver to Salt Lake City, is less than 4,200 ft. above the sea. The train entering is the 'California Zephyr'.

The southern portal of the Lötschberg Tunnel, at Goppenstein, Switzerland. This bore, 9⅛ miles long, is one of the three longest in the Alps, and carries the Lötschberg main line under the main chain of the Bernese Alps from the Rhine watershed to that of the Rhone. The two longest Alpine tunnels are the Gotthard, 9¼ miles, and the Simplon, 12¼ miles; the Italian Apennine Tunnel is 11½ miles long.

the City of London. If you take a tube train at Golder's Green, and travel through to Morden by way of the Bank, you will be underground for no less than 16⅝ miles. But it is, of course, a totally different task to drive 12 feet diameter tunnels through London clay and other soil as compared with blasting a way for a double main line track through the rock of a mountain range.

Much of the London tube tunnelling has been done by great rotary cutters which have propelled themselves forward as they have cut through the soil ahead, while the tunnels themselves have been assembled inside the circular shields in which the cutters work. At every stage of the work it has been possible to know exactly what troubles and difficulties lie ahead; from time to time, too, it has been possible to check, by shafts coming up to the surface, that the tunnels are following precisely the course intended.

But think of starting work on a mountain tunnel from two points perhaps ten miles or so apart. How are we to ensure that when the two bores have been driven towards one another for five miles from each direction, they are certain to meet? Only by the most scrupulously accurate work with the tunnelling theodolites; for once we have started, we have nothing more than the width of the tunnel in which to check that we are moving straight forward. But that is not all, by any means.

In tunnelling it is always the unexpected that happens. At its maximum, a tunnel through a mountain range may be anything from 5,000 to 7,000 feet below the surface, so there is no possibility of driving shafts down from above to the line of the tunnel to ascertain through what kind of rock the tunnel may have to pass. Some of the strata may be 'rotten', and rock of that description, with its tendency to move, may give appalling difficulties. When the Simplon tunnel was being bored, the movement in certain strata pierced by the tunnel was so great that strong steel reinforcements inserted to strengthen the tunnel structure were bent completely out of shape; eventually the tunnel had to be lined through this section with a succession of horseshoe-shaped steel girders, in order to withstand the tremendous pressure from without.

Then there is the constant risk of the bursting into the workings of underground streams, which also can give an immense amount of trouble till means are found to tame them and carry the water out of the workings. One of the worst disasters of this kind occurred when the Lötschberg Tunnel was being bored in Switzerland. Without warning, the bore from the north end of the tunnel broke into an immense underground fissure in the rock, filled with water and glacial debris, which swept into the workings, drowning every man at work at the face, and filling the bore up solidly to a distance of a mile-and-a-half back from where the break-in occurred.

Eventually a massive wall was built inside the tunnel, to shut off the affected length, and three curves were introduced in order to carry the tunnel well clear of the danger area. So today the Lötschberg Tunnel is half-a-mile longer than the straight route originally planned, and, needless to say, cost far more than the original estimate. Marvellous to relate, when the centre-lines met, after nearly five miles of boring in each direction and the insertion of the curves, the error in their meeting was no more than *six inches!*

The Lötschberg, just over nine miles in length, is one of the four longest tunnels in the world, three of which are in, or partly in, Switzerland. It was opened in 1913, and is just beaten in length by the $9\frac{1}{4}$ miles of the Gotthard Tunnel, which is 31 years older. The record is held by the Simplon Tunnel — or tunnels, for there are two single line bores, 56 feet apart — which is just over $12\frac{1}{4}$ miles in length; the first tunnel was brought into use in 1906 and the second in 1921. The runner-up is the Apennine Tunnel of the Italian State Railways, much the youngest of them all, for it was not opened until 1934. Before it was bored, the main Milan–Rome line had to wind its way through the Apennines, between Bologna and Florence, with many sharp curves and steep gradients, and it was decided to cut straight through the mountain range at tremendous cost by what is called a *direttissima* route, involving the boring of this $11\frac{1}{2}$-mile tunnel and various other tunnels as well. Italy also was responsible for the earliest of the long tunnels, called the Mont Cenis (or, more accurately, the Fréjus Tunnel), which is used by trains on the way from Paris to Turin and Rome. This is $8\frac{1}{2}$ miles long and was completed in 1871.

America's longest railway tunnel is the Cascade Tunnel, not far short of 8 miles in length, threaded by the Great Northern Railway on its way to Seattle, on the Pacific Coast. Another American tunnel, the Moffat, is of interest for two reasons; one is that the $6\frac{1}{4}$ miles of its length

The record width of span in Great Britain for a railway arch built of masonry is held by Ballochmyle Viaduct, on the main line of the one-time Glasgow & South Western Railway from Carlisle to Glasgow (St. Enoch). It is situated 11 miles south of Kilmarnock, where the railway crosses the deep valley of the Ayr River. The magnificent central span is 181 ft. across.

were bored at a height of more than 9,000 feet above sea level, and the other is that the 'cut-off' of which it forms a part shortened the Denver & Rio Grande Western main line by no less than 175 miles.

In Great Britain we have no tunnels, other than the tube tunnels already mentioned, that in length come anywhere near the world's longest. Britain's record is held by the Severn Tunnel, which takes the twenty-sixth place on the list. However, the Severn, with its $4\frac{1}{4}$ miles of length, can certainly claim to be the longest under-water railway tunnel in the world.

Those who drove the Severn Tunnel had reason to fear the power of water; the work was held up for long periods by flooding, partly by water breaking down into the workings from above, partly by water overflowing in from both ends when the periodic tidal wave known as the 'Bore' came sweeping up the Severn estuary, but mainly because of the unwelcome attentions of a vast underground flow of water which was called the 'Great Spring'. Even today, powerful pumping machinery, working day and night, clears some 20,000,000 gallons of water daily from the vicinity of the tunnel walls. Nearest rival to the Severn in Great Britain is Totley Tunnel, between Sheffield and Manchester; this is over $3\frac{1}{2}$ miles long, and one of a series of long east-west tunnels that have been driven through the hard rock of the Pennine range.

In running through the darkness of a tunnel, it is not easy, unless you know something of the story of its construction, to picture the triumph, perhaps against almost insuperable odds, of the men who slowly, laboriously, and with astonishing accuracy, drove their way through Nature's obstacles in order to reach their objective. But it is a different matter altogether with the great bridge. The whole of its vast proportions can be seen at once; it stands as a most impressive monument to its designers and builders. As compared with the black hole which is all there is to mark the entrace to a tunnel, however long that tunnel may be, the bridge is something we can look at from end to end, and admire, and marvel at.

In the earliest days of railways, steel was unknown; bridges had therefore to be built with masonry or stone, or cast iron or wrought iron, all of which had their limitations. In Great Britain the most spectacular bridge built in wrought iron and masonry was probably Robert Stephenson's Britannia Tubular Bridge, carrying the Holyhead main line of the then London & North Western Railway across the Menai Straits from North Wales into the island of Anglesey. The railway tracks run through two continuous tubes — technically 'box girders' — each 1,510 feet long, and supported by three great towers; each main span is 459 feet.

A world record for the size of a reinforced concrete span carrying a railway is held by the Lorraine Bridge of the Swiss Federal Railways, at the approach to the main station at Berne. It clears the gorge of the Aar by a single span of no less than 495 ft., carrying four lines of railway.

This was a most remarkable design for its period; the bridge was opened in 1850, and with a certain amount of strengthening work that has been done since, it is still carrying the far heavier traffic of a century later.

The same designer was responsible for another great bridge, opened in 1849 — the original High Level Bridge across the deep valley of the Tyne at Newcastle. This is notable because all its six 125-feet spans are arches of cast iron.

Of masonry arch viaducts there are many of great size which have stood the test of time and vastly increasing loads for over a century. One of these is the Royal Border Bridge, on the East Coast main line south of Berwick, the twenty-eight arches of which carry the East Coast main line 126 feet above the waters of the River Tweed. Biggest of all the masonry arches in Britain that carry railways is one found in south-west Scotland, not far to the south of Kilmarnock on the main line to Carlisle; one main arch of no less than 181 feet span has been thrown across the deep gorge of the River Ayr. It is known as Ballochmyle Bridge.

In later years far bigger structures have been erected in artificial stone — concrete, that is — reinforced by a lattice-work of steel rods. As compared with Ballochmyle's one 181-feet arch, for example, the Delaware, Lackawanna & Western Railroad in the U.S.A. has its great Tunkhannock Viaduct with ten 180-feet arches of reinforced concrete.

The record in concrete structures rests securely with the Swiss Federal Railways. Through the heart of the Swiss capital of Berne there winds the River Aar, deep down in its abruptly-sided valley. For many years the Swiss Federal main lines were carried across this gorge into the main station of Berne by an ugly steel bridge, but this has now been replaced by a magnifi-

TYPES OF BRIDGES

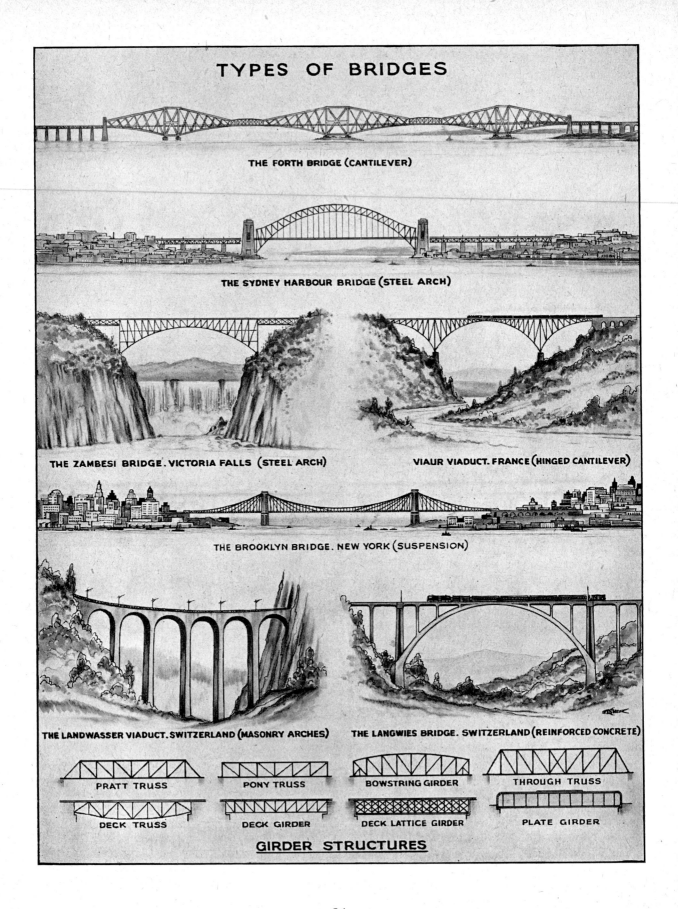

THE FORTH BRIDGE (CANTILEVER)

THE SYDNEY HARBOUR BRIDGE (STEEL ARCH)

THE ZAMBESI BRIDGE. VICTORIA FALLS (STEEL ARCH)

VIAUR VIADUCT. FRANCE (HINGED CANTILEVER)

THE BROOKLYN BRIDGE. NEW YORK (SUSPENSION)

THE LANDWASSER VIADUCT. SWITZERLAND (MASONRY ARCHES)

THE LANGWIES BRIDGE. SWITZERLAND (REINFORCED CONCRETE)

PRATT TRUSS

PONY TRUSS

BOWSTRING GIRDER

THROUGH TRUSS

DECK TRUSS

DECK GIRDER

DECK LATTICE GIRDER

PLATE GIRDER

GIRDER STRUCTURES

In modern bridges of large span, in order to obtain an adequate rise for the arch, the arch is made to rise high into the air, with the bridge floor suspended from it. A remarkable French example of this type of construction, entirely in reinforced concrete, is the Viaduct of the Mediterranean, across the River Rhone south of Lyons. With a span of 394 ft., it is one of the largest of its kind.

cent arch of reinforced concrete, which carries four railway tracks over one great sweeping span of 150 metres — that is, 495 feet.

The world's most spectacular bridges, however, are those which have been carried out in steel. These take various forms. There are the familiar lattice girder bridges, some of which grow to enormous size, as, for example, the Fades Bridge in Central France, which claims to be the highest in the world. It leaps across the valley of the Sioule River in three spans, the widest of them nearly 500 feet in length, and 435 feet above the stream.

Garabit is another notable French bridge, which is of interest because its designer was Eiffel, whose great tower in Paris has made his name known the world over. This is a steel viaduct with one central arch span 540 feet across and 400 feet in height above the River Truyère.

Bigger than either of these, but much less well known, is a third French structure called the Viaur Viaduct, in the south of the country between Rodez and Albi; the 722-feet span of this is the greatest in France.

Viaur has a different method of construction, which is known as the cantilever. This gives maximum strength with a minimum of material by using the principle of balance. A cantilever is usually formed in the shape of a capital 'T', or a diamond set up on one of its points, and so balanced about the centre. A cantilever bridge embodies at least two of these cantilevers; two half-cantilevers, linked together, form the main central span, and the two outer ends of

The world's highest railway bridge is the amazing Fades Viaduct, on the line from Lapeyrouse to Volvic, in Central France. This carries a single track 435 ft. above the Sioule River, in its deep gorge. The central span of this relatively simple structure is 472½ ft. across, and each side span is 380½ ft.; the whole bridge is 1,526 ft. long. Each pier is 303 ft. high, and tapers from 72 ft. by 38 ft. at the base to 36 ft. by 18 ft. at the top.

Centuries ago the Romans knew the art of terracing their bridge structures, in order to obtain greater strength, and there are still remains in both France and Italy of great aqueducts that were built in this terraced fashion. The French railway viaduct of Size, seen in this view, which carries the line from Bourg to Bellegarde across the River Ain, was terraced in order to carry a public road on its lower storey.

36

From time to time it becomes necessary to replace railway bridges built in earlier years, because they are of insufficient strength to carry the constantly increasing weight of locomotives and trains. In this view of the Hawkesbury River Bridge, carrying the Sydney-Newcastle main line of the New South Wales Government Railways, the original bridge, about to be demolished, is on the right, and the new double-track bridge is on the left.

the cantilevers are securely anchored down into rock below the ends of the bridge, forming an immovable whole.

In our own country we have one world-famed cantilever bridge — the Forth Bridge, which crosses the Firth of Forth just to the north of Edinburgh. This immense structure has three cantilevers, the length over which is almost exactly one mile; with the approach viaducts the Forth Bridge measures $1\frac{1}{2}$ miles overall. In this bridge, stability has been obtained by making each cantilever taper outwards towards a broad base. on which its enormous weight stands securely.

Between each pair of cantilevers there is suspended a girder bridge 346 feet across, by means of which each of the two main spans is increased in length to 1,710 feet. These spans are so long that they could leap over the full length of the longest platform of any railway terminus in London, with quite a substantial clearance at both ends. The central cantilever towers to a height of 361 feet, just about equal to the total height above ground of the cross on the dome of St. Paul's Cathedral.

There is only one longer cantilever span in the world carrying a railway, and that is the

Britain's biggest bridge is that which carries the East Coast main line across the Firth of Forth at Queensferry, north of Edinburgh. Each main span is 1,710 ft. across, and the cantilevers reach upwards to 360 ft. above the water level. The total length of bridge and approaches is 1½ miles.

Sydney Harbour Bridge, the most massive in the world, carries four railway tracks, a 60 ft. roadway and two 10 ft. footways by a clear span of 1,650 ft. across Sydney Harbour, New South Wales. A ticklish job was building the great arch out from both sides of the water until the two halves met.

1,800 feet of the Quebec Bridge across the St. Lawrence River in Canada. The building of this bridge was marred by two tragic happenings. The original design was completed in 1901,

The first stage of lifting into position the central section of the 1,800 ft. central span of Quebec Bridge into position; it had been floated to the site on great scows. At the first attempt, a vital link in the hoisting tackle broke, and the 5,100 tons of steel dropped to the bottom of the river. An entirely new central section had to be built, and the second attempt to lift it into position was successful.

and building had been in progress for six years when suddenly, without warning, one of the huge cantilever towers crumpled up, and fell into the river, with the loss of many lives.

An entirely new and much more massive design had then to be prepared, and after the tangled mass of steel had been laboriously cut up, construction recommenced in 1910. By 1916 the two diamond-shaped cantilevers were complete, and nothing remained but to hoist into position the 640-feet central span which was to link the cantilevers together. The span had reached mid-air when once again came disaster; a vital link in the hoisting gear failed, and the 5,100 tons of steel crashed down to the bottom of the river. Not until 1917, sixteen years after building began, was the Quebec Bridge opened for traffic.

What happened to the Quebec Bridge is a reminder that some of the greatest strains to which the members of these great bridges are subjected occur, not when they are carrying their heaviest traffic, but during the work of erection. This was certainly the case with Sydney Harbour Bridge, one of the most remarkable engineering achievements in the world. The vast steel arch which is the essential feature of this bridge, and which towers to 440 feet above the water level, could only be erected by building the two halves of the arch slowly out from the harbour side.

Eventually two great half-arches of latticed steel were projecting out over the harbour for over 820 feet from both sides, each half-arch pressing down on to bearings designed to take a maximum thrust of 19,700 tons apiece, and with four groups of stranded steel cables, 64 in each group, holding on like grim death to the four top corners of the arch. The ticklish job of joining the arch was carried out without a hitch. Today the Sydney Harbour Bridge carries

39

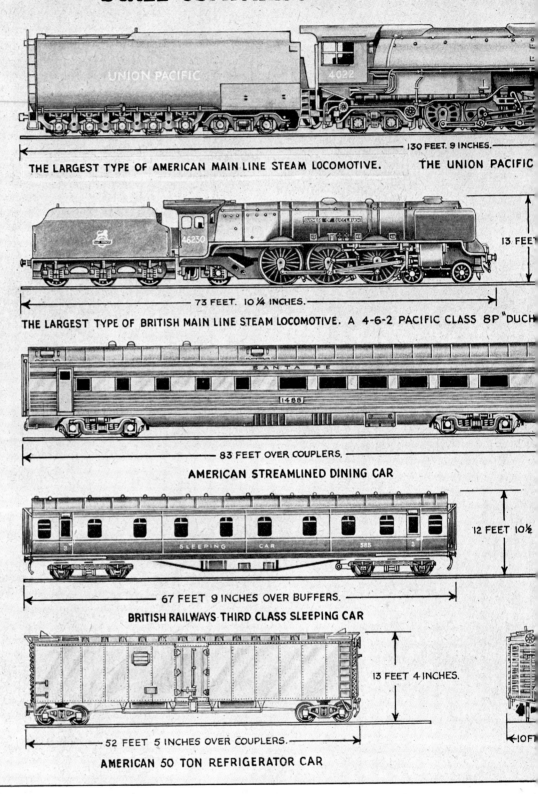

SCALE COMPARISONS OF BRITISH & AM

UNION PACIFIC 4022

130 FEET. 9 INCHES.

THE LARGEST TYPE OF AMERICAN MAIN LINE STEAM LOCOMOTIVE. THE UNION PACIFIC

13 FEET

46230

73 FEET. 10¼ INCHES.

THE LARGEST TYPE OF BRITISH MAIN LINE STEAM LOCOMOTIVE. A 4-6-2 PACIFIC CLASS 8P "DUCH

SANTA FE

1488

83 FEET OVER COUPLERS.

AMERICAN STREAMLINED DINING CAR

12 FEET 10½

SLEEPING CAR 585

67 FEET 9 INCHES OVER BUFFERS.

BRITISH RAILWAYS THIRD CLASS SLEEPING CAR

13 FEET 4 INCHES.

52 FEET 5 INCHES OVER COUPLERS.

10 FT

AMERICAN 50 TON REFRIGERATOR CAR

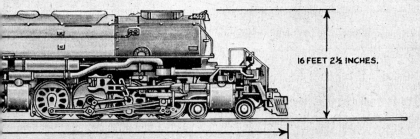

16 FEET 2½ INCHES.

...AD'S 4-8-8-4 SIMPLE MALLET "BIG BOY" CLASS

10 FT. 11 INS.

...ES.

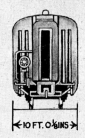

8 FT. 11⅜ INS.

...FEET 9 INCHES.

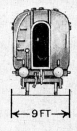

10 FT. 0⅛ INS

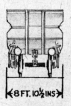

9 FT

9 FEET 10 INCHES.

24 FEET 6 INCHES OVER BUFFERS.

BRITISH RAILWAYS 20 TON COAL WAGON

8 FT. 10½ INS

The Victoria Falls Bridge crosses the gorge of the River Zambesi just below the famous falls. The span of the steel arch is 500 ft., and the single track of the Rhodesia Railways main line, together with a public road, are carried 400 ft. above the river.

Longest railway bridge of its kind in the world is the Huey Long Bridge across the Mississippi River north of New Orleans. In order to obtain sufficient height for vessels to pass under, and to avoid unduly steep gradients, the railway approach viaducts had to begin so far back from the river that the total length of the viaduct and its railway approaches is nearly 4½ miles. The road approaches are shorter and steeper.

across the 1,650 feet width of its span four standard gauge railway tracks, a roadway 57 feet wide, and two ten-feet footways. In all, the floor of this bridge is no less than 160 feet across, and on it four trains, six motor vehicles and many foot passengers can move abreast.

42

There are many longer railway bridges than the famous structures just mentioned. The world's record probably is held by the Huey Long Bridge in Louisiana, U.S.A., which was built to provide the Southern Pacific and other railways with direct access across the wide Mississippi River to the city of New Orleans. To give sufficient clearance for steamers moving up and down the river, long steel approach viaducts were needed to get the trains up to the required level; the entire bridge is all but $4\frac{1}{2}$ miles long.

Opened in 1935, this bridge soon had a rival in the famous Oakland Bay Bridge at San Francisco, also over 4 miles in length in all, and with two of its clear spans each no less than 2,310 feet across. This is a bridge in which the suspension type of construction has been used, but the tracks that it carries are those of tramways and not railways.

Britain's longest bridge is that which crosses the Firth of Tay, immediately south of Dundee; the Tay Bridge has a total length of just over 2 miles. It is closely approached by the 2-mile Störström Bridge in Denmark, built, like its neighbour, the Little Belt Bridge, in order to do away with the necessity for ferrying the trains across the wide waterways separating the mainland of Jutland from the islands which form the remainder of Denmark's European territory. All these are beaten by the 12,064 feet of the Lower Zambesi Bridge in Portuguese East Africa, which carries a 3 feet 6 inch gauge track.

Strictly speaking, Oakland Bay Bridge, linking San Francisco with Oakland, is not a railway bridge, though it carries a long-distance tramway. The two main spans of this bridge, 2,310 ft. each, are beaten by the 4,200 ft. of the adjacent Golden Gate Bridge, another suspension structure; this is the longest single span of any type of bridge in the world. Oakland Bay Bridge cost in all $77,000,000 to build.

CHAPTER 4

The modern steam locomotive

I F you compare a photograph of any large modern steam locomotive with a picture of the kind of engine that hauled the fastest and heaviest trains no more than fifty years ago, you cannot fail to notice how completely locomotive appearance has altered. The long chimney of earlier years has almost vanished; the neat boxes, or 'splashers', that covered the upper parts of driving wheels have gone completely, because the long platform that runs from the buffers back to the cab has been lifted high above the wheels; big sheet steel plates now stand up vertically at the front end of the engine, helping to emphasize its massive appearance; many parts, once concealed inside the locomotive's smooth exterior, have now come out into the

The 'Cornish Riviera Express', Western Region, on its 225½-mile non-stop run from Paddington to Plymouth. The engine is of the 4-cylinder 'King' class, No. 6012 *King Edward VI*; the 'Kings' are the heaviest and most powerful 4–6–0s in Great Britain. The Author is seen leaning out of the cab.

First of the new standard Pacifics of British Railways, No. 70000 *Britannia*. **In power these engines rank as Class '7', and so are inferior to the largest Pacifics of the London Midland, Eastern and South Regions; but they have large boilers and fireboxes, and are capable of hard steaming.**

open, so that their working can be seen; and the whole machine looks vastly more massive and imposing. What are the reasons for all these changes?

Simply put, they are two. One is that you, as a passenger, are always wanting to travel faster and more comfortably; and every increase in both speed and comfort adds to the demand on the locomotive for power. More power means more steam, bigger boilers and bigger cylinders; hence the steadily more massive appearance of the engines. Apart from mere size, however, there are the other changes in outline to which I have referred.

These bring us to the second reason, which is that it pays to make every working part of a locomotive as accessible as possible. In this way inspection and maintenance require less time and labour, because these parts are so much easier to get at than when they were all neatly covered up and boxed in, for the sake of appearances. Unhappily the one-time graceful appearance of the locomotive has suffered in consequence, but we must put up with this, because it is so vital today that all the costs of locomotive working and maintenance should be kept down to the lowest possible figure.

Now while the appearance of locomotives constantly is changing, something else which vitally effects their appearance and their design remains unchanged. Why have locomotive chimneys, and the other mountings on the top of the boiler, been reduced almost to vanishing point? It is because the construction gauge — the maximum height and width to which a locomotive may be built, ruled by the dimensions of bridges, tunnels, platforms, and everything else closely adjacent to the track — does not change.

In the best British main line conditions, no engine must exceed from 13 ft. 5 in. down to

45

The second class in the new British Railways 'family' of standard designs is a light Pacific, in the Class '6' power range, and named after 'Clans'; the first of them is No. 72000 *Clan Buchanan*. Their relatively light and well distributed weight means that they have a wide radius of action. The 'Clans' were intended originally for the heavily graded Highland main line between Perth and Inverness, but began service elsewhere in Scotland.

13 ft. 1 in. (according to Region) from rail to top of chimney in height, and 9 ft. in width. If the engine is to be allowed to run anywhere, because some lines have narrower clearances than others, it may be necessary to keep the height down to as little as 12 ft. 9 in. and the width down to 8 ft. 8 in. The famous Southern 'Schools' are not more than 8 ft. 6½ in. wide, because they were designed to be able to go through some very narrow tunnels on the Tonbridge and Hastings line.

Now try to imagine some of the difficulties of the designer as he tries to increase the size and power of his locomotives. More power, as we have seen, needs more steam; to generate more steam he needs a boiler of bigger diameter, somewhere between 6 ft. and 7 ft., perhaps, at its maximum. But the wheels have to run on a track of which the rails are no more than 4 ft. 8½ in. apart. So the boiler must be lifted high enough to clear the big driving wheels; but then the designer is cramped severely by those narrow limits of height.

There are the same close limits in width; cylinders, bolted to the outsides of the main frames, must not be more than a certain diameter, or they will scrape the platforms. It is a puzzle indeed to stow within the British loading gauge all the working parts of a locomotive capable of exerting more than 3,000 horse-power, for such may be the maximum power demand on the locomotive of today.

Other countries have been farseeing enough to leave more room round their tracks than we have. In the United States, for example, engines up to 15 ft. 6 in. high are common, and in exceptional cases up to 16 ft.; while American railways have up to 10 ft. 6 in. in width with which to play. But notwithstanding these generous limits, the demands on American locomotives for power output are so great that the latest steam locomotives in that country have

The most extensively built locomotive classes today are those designed for 'mixed traffic', with medium-sized driving wheels for heavy freight haulage, but able also to run fast with passenger trains; their days thus can be filled up usefully with a variety of duties. This is a Class '5' 4–6–0 of British Railways, No. 73000, with 6 ft. driving wheels, standard counterpart of the numerous London Midland Class '5s' and the Eastern Region 'B1' 4–6–0s.

been developed to the utmost limits that even 15 ft. 6 in. by 10 ft. 6 in. will permit. The record in the United States is held by the so-called 'Big Boy' freight locomotives of the Union Pacific, vast giants of the 4–8–8–4 wheel arrangement, which with their 14-wheel tenders weigh no less than 540 tons in full running order — three times the weight, the size, and the power of the biggest in Britain.

Over various subsidiary lines and branches locomotives must be restricted in weight, because track and bridges are not up to the heaviest standards. British Railways therefore have introduced a lighter 4–6–0 'mixed traffic' class, of which No. 75000 is an example. As these engines are intended for lighter duties also, the driving wheels are reduced in diameter to 5 ft. 8 in., and a tender of smaller capacity is attached. This engine is in power Class '4'.

For still lighter work, the leading bogie is replaced by a two-wheel pony truck, and the locomotive becomes a 2-6-0, or Mogul, instead of a 4-6-0. No. 76000 is the first 2-6-0 type in the British Railways standard family; it has the same boiler, cylinders, wheels, motion and tender as the Class '4' 4-6-0, in accordance with the principle of making as many as possible of the parts of various classes interchangeable.

The matter of wheel arrangement, mentioned in the last paragraph, needs a little further attention. No doubt you are familiar with the simple Whyte notation, by which the order of the wheels is expressed in figures — the first figure for 'idle' or carrying wheels at the leading end of the engine, the middle figure for driving wheels, and the last figure for carrying wheels at the rear end.

Most express locomotives have a swivelling truck, or 'bogie', at the leading end, to guide the locomotive smoothly round the curves, giving us '4' for the first figure; then follow '4', '6', '8', according to whether the locomotive has four, six, or eight driving wheels coupled (or possibly more); and the final figure may be '2' or '4', if there is a two-wheel or a four-wheel truck at the rear end, or 'o', if the rear pair of driving wheels is directly under the driver's cab. For example, the latest standard 'Britannia' class engines are of the 4–6–2 type; a Western Region 'King' or a London Midland 'Royal Scot' is a 4–6–0; a Southern 'School' is a 4–4–0; and in mixed traffic and freight service there are large numbers of 2–8–0, 2–6–0 and 0–6–0 locomotives.

Why is it necessary to couple the driving wheels of a locomotive together? In earlier days many express engines — as, for example the famous Stirling 'eight-footers' of the one-time Great Northern Railway — were content with one big single pair of driving wheels. Today, as we have seen, they may have two, three or four pairs of equal size, and sometimes even more. The explanation is that if the full power of a modern locomotive were to be applied to a single pair of driving wheels, they would simply spin round uselessly on the rails, through lack of sufficient grip, or adhesion. By the coupling of two or more axles together, they are made to act in unison, and the adhesion is therefore doubled, trebled or quadrupled, as the case may be.

The use of tank engines, carrying their supplies of coal and water on their own main frames, instead of in a separate tender, is confined mainly to Great Britain. No. 80010 is one of the British Railways standard 2-6-4 tanks, capable of fast and heavy work over fairly long distances. Engines of this type are used on the express services over the one-time Cheshire Lines route between Manchester Central and Liverpool Central.

Today, generally speaking, express engines need at least three axles coupled, or six-coupled wheels; in the United States, Canada, and elsewhere, eight-coupled wheels are common even in passenger work. Freight engines for heavy work seldom have less than eight coupled wheels, and in other countries ten-coupled engines are used frequently. The Union Pacific Railroad, U.S.A., goes further with some enormous 4–12–2 locomotives — that is, with six coupled axles, or twelve-coupled wheels. Engines for high speed work have the biggest driving wheels, and those for heavy and slow freight the smallest.

For shunting work, a smaller water and coal capacity is needed, and the 0-6-0 wheel arrangement suffices for most needs. No. 9400 is a typical Western Region type, carrying its water in raised 'pannier' tanks, instead of the more usual flat side tanks; this arrangement makes it easier to obtain access to the motion work under the boiler. In earlier days the Great Western used many 'saddle' tanks, with their water supply astride the boiler.

The Garratt method of articulation makes it possible to spread the weight of a powerful locomotive over a lengthy wheelbase. The large diameter boiler of 2-6-6-2 No. 47995, London Midland Region, is carried on a girder frame which transmits its weight to two 2-6-0 chassis, each with its own cylinders and motion. Each chassis is pivoted under the ends of the frame, so that the lengthy locomotive can adjust itself to the curves.

In a previous paragraph we thought of the Union Pacific 'Big Boy' class locomotives, and noted that their wheel arrangement is 4–8–8–4. Why the *fourth* figure? This introduces us to a principle known as 'articulation'. We have seen how, owing to the limitations of the loading gauge, it is impossible to make locomotives taller or wider, in our search for more power. The only possible alternative, therefore, is to make them longer.

This development might not present so much difficulty if all the track were straight; but locomotives have to be designed in such a way that they can pass readily round curves. Moreover, in mountain country, where maximum power often is needed because of the steepness of the gradients, the curves may be very sharp as well. Articulation gets over this difficulty by providing a locomotive that is very lengthy, but without any sacrifice of flexibility. An articulated engine, in effect, is two locomotives in one, supplied with steam from one boiler and manned by one crew.

At various points on the Midland main line of the London Midland Region, but especially between the big marshalling sidings at Cricklewood, in North London, and Toton, near Nottingham, you may see working a number of engines which arrest attention immediately by their curious appearance. In the centre they have a large boiler, carried on a frame which resembles a girder bridge, for it has no wheels beneath it. Supporting the two ends of this frame there are two 2–6–0 chassis, each with its own cylinders and motion. If you were to look carefully at these chassis as the engine passes round a sharp curve, you would realize that the connection between the chassis and the frame is a pivot, and that each chassis, independent of the other, is swinging as it takes the curve. The reason why the boiler has to be carried above a space between the two sets of wheels is that it is too big to be mounted above them without fouling the bridges over the line. But this arrangement also has the advantage of spreading the weight of a very powerful locomotive over a considerable length of track, so that less strain is imposed on the track and the bridges as it moves along.

The articulated locomotive need be very little longer than an ordinary locomotive, because the former has no separate tender to carry its supplies; water is carried in big tanks above each chassis, and the water tank at the cab end of the locomotive has above it a capacious coal bunker. In the London Midland Region articulated locomotives, mentioned in the last paragraph (which, by the way, are of the 2–6–6–2 type), the coal is stored in a big inclined cylinder, which rotates while the engine is running, so causing the coal to slide downwards towards the fireman, and helping him with his hard work.

Very much bigger articulated engines can be found in all parts of the United States, where the additional height available above the tracks makes it possible to mount their enormous boilers directly above the wheels. We have thought already of the Union Pacific 4–8–8–4 'Big Boys'; then there are 4–6–6–4's, 2–6–6–6's (a most unusual wheel arrangement, on the Chesapeake & Ohio Railroad, on engines with fireboxes of such huge size that they need a six-wheel bogie to carry them), 2–8–8–4's, 4–8–8–2's, and so on.

The Southern Pacific has a number of 4–8–8–2 locomotives of curious design, in which the driver's cab comes first, the chimney is at the rear end, and the tender trails behind that. They are used in California, where the oil wells are, and are fired with oil instead of coal; the oil is piped from the tender along the side of the engine to the firebox at the front end, so that

In a compound locomotive, the steam is carried through two stages of expansion, first in a high pressure cylinder or cylinders, and then in two low pressure cylinders. The only such engines in Great Britain today are the well-known three-cylinder compounds of the London Midland Region, which originated on the Midland Railway. No. 1002 (since renumbered 41002) is seen hauling an express from Leeds to Morecambe.

the engine crew have a magnificent look-out, with nothing to obstruct the view, and are kept completely away from the smoke and fumes that come out of the engine chimney. Oil-firing is common enough in countries which, like the United States, have their own supplies of oil, but in Great Britain oil needs to be imported, so that coal-firing is the cheaper method of the two.

American locomotives have appetites proportionate to their enormous size and power. The tenders that they need to keep them supplied with coal and water would astonish you if you could see them. The biggest British tenders, such as those of the 'Pacific' locomotives of the Eastern and North Eastern Regions, are carried on eight wheels and accommodate 5,000 gallons of water and between 9 and 10 tons of coal. The largest American tenders need fourteen or sixteen wheels for their support; water capacities of 20,000 to 25,000 gallons are common, and as to coal, the latest 14-wheel tender of the New York Central 'Niagara' class 4–8–4 locomotives held no less than 41 tons! Tenders such as those just mentioned, when fully charged with coal and water, weigh all but 200 tons apiece; each tender, that is to say, turns the scale at more than the biggest *locomotive and tender* in Great Britain.

You will be familiar with the fact that many locomotives in Great Britain, for the most part used on relatively short journeys or in shunting, have no separate tenders at all. In front of the cab, and along both sides of the boiler, there are flat box-shaped structures; these are the water tanks, and locomotives of this type usually are known as 'tank engines', to distinguish

The French have always specialized in compound propulsion for locomotives, and No. 232.U.1 of the S.N.C.F. (French National Railways) is a magnificent example of their modern practice. It has two high-pressure and two low-pressure cylinders, and is used on express services from Paris (Nord) to Lille, and also on Paris-Brussels expresses. The wheel arrangement is 4-6-4, and the semi-streamlined front end will be noted.

North American locomotives in general are vastly bigger than anything in Great Britain, such as this 2-10-4 'Selkirk' type engine of the Canadian Pacific Railway, designed to work heavy passenger and freight trains over the 5,335 ft. summit of the Great Divide, in the Rockies west of Calgary. The steepest approach gradients are at 1 in 45. But these fine engines have now been displaced by the all-conquering diesels that are now flooding North American railways.

them from 'tender engines'. The coal is stored in a bunker at the rear of the cab. Some shunting engines, such as those used on the Western Region, carry their water supply in a tank above the boiler; if this is curved on top to a radius similar to that of the boiler barrel, it is called a 'saddle tank', but if it is flat on top it is known as a 'pannier tank', because the boiler, when seen end on, looks rather like an animal carrying a couple of panniers on its back.

So the tank locomotive is completely self-contained; it carries its supplies on its own main frames. But they are smaller supplies, of course, than those of the tender engine, as they do not need to last for so long continuously. No other countries make such extensive use of tank engines as Great Britain.

Earlier in this chapter I mentioned the fact that a British locomotive designer is limited in the size of the cylinders that he can mount outside his engine, if the outsides of the cylinders are to clear the platforms alongside which they must pass. In the engines of fifty years ago, the cylinders were almost always fitted inside the engine, out of sight, between the main frames which you can see extending like two knife-edges from beneath the boiler to the front buffer-beam. This inside arrangement was thought to enable an engine to run more steadily, as well as helping towards the neat appearance of locomotives, of which so much was thought in Great Britain in days gone by. But it had disadvantages. One was that the driving axle had to be 'cranked' — that is, formed into a double 'U' shape — so that it might be capable of being turned by the connecting rods; you know, of course, that the pistons in the cylinders, driven to and fro by the steam, communicate their motion through cross-heads to the connecting rods, the 'big ends' of which turn the driving wheels by means of the cranks. Also this arrangement meant that cylinders and motion were not nearly so easy to get at for inspection and repair as if they were outside the engine.

So the modern preference is entirely for cylinders outside the engine, where you can see exactly how the connecting rods turn the driving wheels by means of crank-pins. You notice also the arrangement of steel rods, with its curious motion, that extends backwards from the driving wheels towards the cylinders: this is the 'valve-motion' or 'valve-gear'. It terminates in a rod, parallel to the piston rod, that passes into a smaller cylinder above the cylinder proper.

The smaller cylinder is the 'valve-chest', and it houses the 'piston-valve', which has the all-important task of letting the steam into the cylinder at precisely the right moment, and

Capacious tenders must be provided to match the appetites of the large North American locomotives. This 12-wheeled Canadian National example, carries 11,000 gallons of water and 20 tons of coal. The barrel-shaped water tank is cheaper to build than a tender with flat sides. Some U.S.A. tenders are mounted on 14 and even 16 wheels.

then releasing it, when it has done its work of expanding and pushing the piston either forward or backward. After release, the spent steam, or 'exhaust', as it is called, passes up through the blast-pipe into the chimney, from which it emerges as the succession of puffs — each one of them a cylinder-full of spent steam — that make so characteristic a sound when the steam locomotive is in motion. We shall hear some more about the valve motion in the next chapter.

With the most powerful modern engines there is not sufficient room to mount, either inside the frames or outside, two cylinders of big enough diameter to develop the power required from the engine. With articulated engines, as we have seen, there are four cylinders, one pair at each end of the engine, and all four outside. But there are also ordinary locomotives with four cylinders, two outside and two inside, like the Western Region 'Kings' and 'Castles', for example, or the big 'Duchess' and 'City' Pacifics of the London Midland Region.

Other Regions have favoured three-cylinder engines, with two outside cylinders and one inside, like the streamlined Pacifics used on the Eastern Region 'Flying Scotsman' and other expresses, or the London Midland 'Royal Scots' or the Southern 'Schools'. You can always recognize a three-cylinder engine by the way in which you hear six puffs, instead of four, every time the driving wheels rotate. Normally with four-cylinder engines, however, the puffs are thrown out in pairs, so that there are only four puffs to a revolution, as with a two-cylinder engine.

One more note may conclude this chapter. In the previous paragraph I referred to a 'Pacific'. This is the nickname, imported from America, given to the 4–6–2 arrangement of wheels. A 4–4–2 is an 'Atlantic'; a 2–6–2 an engine of the 'Prairie' type; a 2–6–0 a 'Mogul'; a 2–8–0 a 'Consolidation': to mention the best-known of these nicknames. But the notation — 4–6–2, 4–6–0, 2–6–2, 2–6–0, 2–8–0, 0–6–0, and so on — is much the simplest and most exact way of describing a locomotive in terms that admit of no misunderstanding.

It is remarkable indeed that a locomotive of such size as No. 3268 of the South African Railways can have been developed on a track gauge no wider than 3 ft. 6 in. The slightly larger Class '15F' engines, also with the 4-8-2 wheel arrangement, weigh 109 tons apiece, and their tenders 68½ tons, making a total of 177½ tons, as compared with the 163 tons of a British 'Duchess' Pacific of the London Midland Region.

1. Guard iron.
2. Coupling.
3. Footstep.
4. Buffer.
5. Vacuum brake connection.
6. Lamp iron.
7. Inside piston-valve tail rod casings.
8. Steam pipe casing.
9. Smoke deflector.
10. Smoke box door.

11. Smoke box door lock and clamp.
12. Double chimney.
13. Superheater header.
14. Main steam pipe to cylinders.
15. Double blast pipe.
16. Exhausts from all four cylinders.
17. Exhaust pipe from ejector.
18. Feed-water clack valves.
19. Regulator valve at entry to main steam pipe.

20. Regulator shaft (to regulator handle in cab).
21. Safety valves and whistle over firebox (not visible).
22. Firebox stays.
23. Cab.
24. Firebox.
25. Firehole door.
26. Brick arch.
27. Splasher.

COMOTIVE 'DUCHESS OF ATHOLL'

28. Sand-box fillers.
29. Mechanical lubricators.
30. Boiler casing.
31. Fire tubes from firebox to smokebox.
32. Piston-valve chest.
33. Cylinder relief valve.
34. Main frame.
35. Piston.
36. Outside cylinder.

37. Cylinder drains.
38. Leading bogie.
39. Walschaerts valve gear.
40. Slide bar.
41. Cross-head.
42. Radius rod.
43. Expansion link.
44. Connecting rod.
45. Eccentric rod.
46. Brake blocks.

47. Coupling rod.
48. Counterweight.
49. Steam sand pipes.
50. Rear end of main frame.
51. Axle box of trailing Bissel truck.
52. Exhaust steam injector.
53. Coal capacity, 10 tons.
54. Water capacity, 4,000 gallons.
55. Water uptake from pick-up scoop.

CHAPTER 5

The locomotive at home and at work

As every locomotive spotter knows, the 'iron horse', like the horse of flesh and blood, is attached to a stable. In earlier days this was known as a 'shed'; today, when we have become more precise and more technical, it is called a 'motive power depot'. This is where the locomotive lives; here it is fed and watered; here it is groomed and receives any necessary 'medical' attention to keep it in good running order; and to the depot there are attached, not only the 'grooms' and the 'doctors', but also the men to whose care the locomotive is entrusted as it leaves its home to set about its day's work.

One of these depots is an interesting place. As we approach, the first thing to catch our eye, probably, is a tall coaling plant, under which the engines move to obtain their supplies of

A motive power depot, at which locomotives are stabled, and receive their day-to-day inspection and maintenance. At the entrance to the shed roads are seen the pits over which the engines stand, so that the fitters may be able to get underneath; to the right is the coaling tower. This particular shed is at Carnforth, near Lancaster.

A LOCOMOTIVE COALING PLANT

(1) Machinery house. (2) Outer stairway. (3) Cable winding drums worked by (4) 30 horse-power electric motor fitted with magnetic brake. (5) Wagon cradle counterweights. (6) Hood. (7) Counterweight guides. (8) Hand winch for operating two-way flap. (9) Gallery. (10) Receiving bunker. (11) Two-way flap which can be operated to close the opening of one or other of the two storage bunkers, thus enabling coal to be shot into the one left open. (12) Gallery. (13) Bulkhead dividing storage bunkers. (14) Reinforced concrete structure. (15) Anti-breakage trunks. (16 & 17) Storage bunkers, each 75 tons capacity. These bunkers allow for two grades or qualities of coal to be stored ready for feeding to locomotives as required. (18) Hoisting cables. (19) Exterior gallery. (20) Water pipe connected to sprays for damping down coal dust during operations. (21) Coal being gravity fed to jig feeder. (22) 5 horse-power electric motors for operating jig feeders. (23) Three-way flap which can be controlled to regulate the feeding of coal to the tender. (24) Operating shaft and linkages for three-way flap. (25) Tender of locomotive on coaling road receiving supply of coal. (26) Meter automatically recording amount of coal supplied. (27) Operator's cabins. (28) Control cabin. (29) Coal wagon in position on cradle. (30) Cradle runways. (31) Wagon road. (32) Wagon cradle. The wagon is hoisted bodily upon this into hood (6) where it automatically tilts, tipping its contents into receiving bunker (10). (33) Concrete-lined pit.

A modern motive power depot of the 'round shed' type, at Old Oak Common, Western Region. The engine tracks all radiate from a central turntable; an engine thus can be got out of the shed without moving a number of others, but a shed of this type requires more space than one of the more usual kind, with parallel tracks. The suspended cowls are to carry away the smoke from the engine chimneys.

fuel. In the more modern of these plants, coal wagons are lifted bodily by hydraulic or electric hoists to the top of the tower, and there are turned over bodily, so that their contents are discharged into the great bunker of steel or reinforced concrete that forms the central part of the plant. As each engine moves under the bunker, the underside doors are opened by electric push-button control, and a mass of coal drops down on to the tender, controlled according to the quantity needed, and automatically weighed and recorded. So a task which used to be done slowly and laboriously with hand-manipulated baskets now is completed in one or two minutes.

Inside the depot we find the engines standing over long inspection pits, so designed that fitters and engine-crews can get underneath the locomotives, and give the close inspection that is necessary. From time to time boilersmiths have to examine the insides of the boilers — a by no means easy task that calls for the use of electric lamps and small mirrors. Boilers need to have scraped all the surfaces which normally have fire on one side and water on the other — the former of deposits of soot and the latter of scale, both of which are bad conductors of heat and will prevent the boiler from steaming properly. Brakes may need adjustment or new brake-blocks; wasted firebars may require replacement; and a thousand-and-one other jobs require attention.

Some of the tasks of locomotive maintenance need to be carried out only at intervals; others must be given attention once every twenty-four hours. If the locomotive in running continuously over a long distance — as, for example, over 299 miles non-stop between London (Euston) and Carlisle, London Midland Region — it cannot get back to its home depot the same day, and so is required to be a 'boarder' at the depot at the far end of its run, returning the following day. The same applies to engine crews, for whose use a number of comfortable hostels are provided at various important locomotive centres.

It is a long ladder that leads ultimately to locomotive driving. The first rung is locomotive cleaning; during this part of the climb the boy who has entered railway service learns all about locomotives, how they are built, what purpose is served by their many different parts, and so on. After a year or two at cleaning there comes promotion to be a fireman — much quicker in these days of shortage of staff than ever it was in days gone by. Up the ladder the young fireman makes his way, rung by rung — a shunting engine first, then a freight or a suburban passenger engine, and then, at last, an express engine.

During his years of firing, he is learning, from watching the drivers with whom he works, the right methods of handling locomotives; he is also getting a thorough grasp of the routes over which he works, their gradients, signals, and so on; and he is mastering the many rules laid down for the safe working of the trains.

The time has now come for the fireman to be 'passed' as a driver. Still there are numerous

With the increase in the size of modern locomotives, turning them end-for-end has become a considerable problem. The 2-10-4 Canadian Pacific 'Selkirk' type locomotive, shown here in course of turning at Field, B.C., measures 97 ft. 11 in. overall, and so requires a turntable of 100 ft. diameter. In the United States there are even longer locomotives, up to a maximum of 117 ft. 7 in., and where possible a triangle of lines, or 'wye', is used for turning.

While streamlining of a locomotive is an asset, if it is to be used for high-speed passenger service, it is disadvantageous from the maintenance point of view, as the casing must be removed whenever external boiler inspection is required. The train shown is the pre-war 'Coronation Scot', headed L.M.S.R. by streamlined Pacific No. 6224 *Princess Alexandra*, at speed on its southbound journey near Penrith.

rungs of the ladder to be climbed — shunting engine, freight engine, slow passenger engine, and, finally, express passenger engine. To be a driver in the 'top link' at the depot (the set of drivers and firemen who are responsible for the most important and most remunerative duties), is the top rung of the ladder. By now, the driver is a man with many years of experience behind him, an expert in the handling of a locomotive; and getting the best out of a modern engine, with due regard to the weight and speed of the train, the gradients and the timetable, is a highly scientific task. Coupled with it is the unceasing vigilance needed to help in maintaining the railways' proud record of safe travel.

And now the time has come to join a driver and fireman one day as they arrive at the depot in readiness to take over their locomotive for a day's duty. About an hour before their engine is due to leave the shed they come walking in, and make first for the duty board, where they find posted up all the day's duties — the men's names, the engines they are to man, the trains they are to work, and so on.

Next comes the business of 'booking on duty', and after that a scrutiny of the notice board, which gives them 'stop press' information as to any special matters to be noted, as, for example, that sudden repairs have become necessary to a certain stretch of track, over which they will have to reduce speed, or that no water will be available at a certain station at which they had expected to take some. The majority of such information, however, is given in the printed 'Weekly Working Notice', of which each driver has a copy.

Following this there is the drawing of 'stores' — lubricating oil, lamps, shovel, and so on — which will be needed for the journey. The fire in the engine is alight, of course; boys are detailed at the shed specially to attend to the lighting of engine fires at the right time, so that there is a fair pressure of steam in the boiler before the crew take over. Often the fire is not allowed to go out while the engine is at the shed; it is cleaned of ash and clinker, and kept low until shortly before the next day's duty begins, when the engine 'blower' is put on, to make an artificial draught, and the pressure begins to creep up once again.

For some time the driver and fireman are busily engaged in going round their engine, examining all the working parts, attending to the lubrication, and so on. At last everything is in readiness. The engine moves majestically out of the shed; there is a pause at the water column while the tender tank is filled to the top; a brief wait ensues till the signal which allows exit from the depot to the main line is pulled off; and along this the locomotive proceeds, tender first, to the the terminus.

There, at one of the main departure platforms, the express is waiting. With the skill born of constant practice, the driver backs down so gently that passengers in the train feel not a vestige of shock as the buffers of the tender touch those of the leading coach. The fireman has now to get down on to the platform, and then to drop into the narrow space between tender and train, in order to 'couple up'.

Another important duty is to join together the ends of the flexible hose-pipes which form the braking system of the train, and enable the driver, on the footplate, by means of a vacuum principle, to apply the brakes on every pair of wheels from the front of the train to

In order to simplify maintenance, for the reason given under the illustration opposite, the streamline casings have now been stripped off the London Midland Pacifics which previously carried them, as No. 46223 *Princess Alice*, here seen climbing the 1 in 75 of Shap incline with the down 'Royal Scot'. The de-streamlined engines can always be recognized by the downward slope of the smokebox top ahead of the chimney.

AN ENGINE CREW'S DAY

(I)

At the start of his working day, the driver makes his way to the motive power depot to which he is attached, in this case Old Oak Common shed of the Western Region.

The first task of driver and fireman is to book on duty. The time at which they are required to do so leaves ample margin for preparatory work before the engine leaves the shed.

Next, the roster board must be consulted. It tells the crew which engine and train they are to man, where the engine is standing in the shed, and by what train they will return.

The notice-board must now be scrutinized. It sets out any emergency conditions affecting the running, such as special speed restrictions, shortage of water at any particular station, and so on.

Part of the engine preparation consists in emptying the smokebox of any ashes left after the last run, which might hinder steaming. This is done by a member of the shed staff.

The driver now goes all round the engine, oiling all motion parts, seeing that all oil-boxes are full and adjusting trimmings, and trying the fit of nuts and cotters, to see that all is secure.

AN ENGINE CREW'S DAY (II)

Meantime the fireman has been busy, collecting shovel, bucket, spanners and oil from the stores, trimming the coal forward to the tender front, and seeing that the tender tank is filled.

At last, after 45 to 60 minutes preparation, No. 6001 *King Edward VII* is ready, and moves majestically out of the shed yard, tender first, to make its way to Paddington.

After the engine has backed on to the train, the fireman couples up, and then drops in position on the engine's front buffer-beam the two white headlamps which indicate 'Express Passenger Train'.

Leaning out of the cab and looking down the platform, the fireman waits for the whistle and waving of the guard's green flag which will be the signal to give 'Right Away' to the driver.

The driver in his working position on the footplate. His right hand is on the lever by which the 'cut-off' is adjusted and the engine reversed; his left hand is on the brake-valve.

There is little respite for the fireman during the journey. His business is to see that the steam pressure is kept near 'blowing off' point and that the boiler is kept full of water.

The formidable array of appliances in the cab of a Canadian National 4-8-4 express locomotive. The driver, or 'engineer', as he is called in North America, is seated on the right. Above his head is the quadrant-plate in which the regulator handle moves; the lever of the reversing gear is behind him, and his left hand is on the brake-valve. There is no firehole door, as the firing is done mechanically, by worm and screw feed from the tender; the fireman is able to adjust the rate of feed from his seated position.

the back. High speeds would not be safely possible but for this use of 'continuous' brakes, which make it possible to stop a train in a very short distance in case of emergency.

Shortly before the start, the guard strides up the platform to the engine, so that he may enter in his book the engine number and the names of the engine crew. The three men have known each other for years, probably, and exchange greetings; the guard returns to the rear of the train, and all is in readiness for the start. On the stroke of time, the station master or the platform inspector gives the guard a signal; the fireman, leaning out from the cab, over the heads of the people on the platform sees the guard's green flag being waved; and across the cab to the driver he signals the 'right away'. The latter has been keeping his eye on the platform starting signal, and having assured himself that it is in the 'clear' position, he opens the engine regulator.

Powerful modern locomotives need the most careful handling as they are being started.

The regulator handle is a prominent object in the driver's cab. As the driver moves it, he is opening the valve, usually located in the 'dome', a space above the boiler barrel in which steam collects well above the water level — covered by the casing that looks like a bowler hat in shape — that permits live steam to enter the main steam pipe. If the driver opens the valve too far at first, so much steam rushes down to the cylinders that the power suddenly applied causes the driving wheels to slip round uselessly on the rails, to the accompaniment of a fusillade of puffs from the engine chimney. To forestall this possible slipping, the driver has not only opened his regulator cautiously, but if you look down at the driving wheels, you will see that he is applying sand between the wheels and the rails, usually with the help of a blast of steam, to improve the grip or adhesion.

As the engine gets into motion, you will notice that the driver pushes the regulator handle further and further over, until, perhaps, he has pushed it as far as it will go; the regulator now is full open. But if you have been watching closely, you will have seen him doing something else at the same time. He has been turning a wheel that stands in front of him, bit by bit, and as

The cab of this modern British Standard locomotive, with its party of juniors being shown how everything works, provides an interesting contrast with the Canadian cab opposite. The regulator handle is seen vertically immediately behind the guide's arm, with the brake-valve to the left of it. A boy is sitting in the driver's seat, with the reversing gear in front of him (out of sight). On the right is the fireman's seat.

67

The immense size of a modern American locomotive can be grasped by comparing the size of the man in the cab with what is seen of Canadian National 4-8-4 No. 6100. Five or six steps are needed from ground level to reach the footplate. This Canadian cab is completely closed in, to protect the crew from cold winter temperatures.

he turns it, the needle of an indicator is gradually falling from the '75' mark, or thereabouts, at which it started, to '20' or even '15'. These figures indicate percentages of 'cut-off'.

You will remember that in the previous chapter we noticed the arrangement of rods in front of the coupled wheels, called the 'valve-motion', which controls the admission of the steam to the cylinders, and its release when it has done its work. The valve-motion does something else. By its action, the entrance of steam into the cylinder is cut off when the piston has completed part of its travel; for the rest of the piston travel, or 'stroke', as it is called, the steam is doing its work of pushing by expansion. The more this property of expansion can be used, so much more work can the same weight of steam be made to do, and so much more efficient does the working of the locomotive become.

On starting, we needed the maximum 'push' of the pistons possible, without slipping the wheels, so steam was admitted during almost the whole of the piston stroke (75 per cent cut-off). Then the cut-off was gradually brought back — 'notching up', the enginemen call it — until perhaps steam was being admitted to the cylinders for no more than one-seventh part of the stroke (15 per cent), and for the remaining six-sevenths has been doing its work by expansion. This explains why the modern express engine is so quiet in its working at high speed; as the steam expands, so its pressure drops, and by the time it is thrown away out of the chimney, there is very little pressure left. This makes for increased efficiency, because all power that is thrown away, no matter how little, is wasted power. Why should any be wasted at all?

To answer this question, we need to transfer our attention for a time from the driver to the fireman, who is busily engaged in shovelling coal from the tender across the footplate and through the firehole door into the glowing furnace within. Now watch as he throws that next

68

Construction of a British Railways Pacific locomotive in progress. Extending backwards from the front buffer-beam, like knife-edges, are the main frames; bolted to them on the outside are the two cylinders, with their piston-valve chests above. Between the cylinders is the curved saddle for the support of the smokebox. Note the strong bracings between the frames.

Front end of a locomotive that has been prepared for testing. The shelter built round the smokebox is to provide protection for two observers who, with an appliance called an indicator, will diagram the exact course of the expansion of the steam in the cylinders. From these diagrams it can be seen if the locomotive is using its steam efficiently or not.

shovelful in. Look through one of the front windows of the cab, and at the same moment you will see a puff of black smoke mixing with the exhaust steam that is pouring from the chimney. What has just taken place in the firebox, in which the fire is blazing, has affected what is going on in the smokebox, at the other end of the boiler barrel.

If you can stand the heat, peer through the flames, when the firehole door is open, and at the opposite end of the firebox you will see hundreds of small holes. Had the big door at the front of the smokebox, between the buffers and the chimney, been open while we were in the engine shed, you would have seen a corresponding number of holes at the other end of the boiler barrel. These holes are the ends of the fire-tubes, which make an open passage through the barrel of the boiler direct from the firebox to the smokebox.

It is not difficult to realize what is happening. The spent steam, shooting upwards from the cylinders through the upright blast-pipe (which occupies the centre of the smokebox) to the chimney creates a strong suction. It is this suction that is drawing air through the blazing mass of coal, and is giving it all the oxygen that it needs for combustion; then the tremendously hot gases that are produced by this combustion are being drawn through the tubes into the smokebox, where they pass out of the chimney with the steam. That is why we saw the puff of black smoke from the chimney immediately after the fireman had put his shovelful of coal on the fire.

So we learn the secret of the amazing rapidity with which the relatively small locomotive boiler can generate steam. The most steam is being made in the water space that surrounds the firebox, but all the fire-tubes, encased with water and filled with the hot gases, are making steam also, while at the same time permitting the draught that causes the fire to blaze so fiercely.

Looking narrowly into the firebox, we may notice that some of the holes are larger than the remainder. These are the 'flues', and if we could look inside them we should find in them nests of small tubes containing steam. This is a reminder that, when the driver opens the regulator, the steam does not pass directly to the cylinders; it has a long journey to make first. It is conducted to and fro, in those superheater tubes, getting gradually hotter and hotter; the hotter it is when the time comes to use it — though for reasons which it is difficult to explain in simple terms — so much more efficiently the locomotive is likely to work.

As we ride with the engine crew, we notice the mass of equipment that faces them. Very important are two vertical glass tubes called 'water-gauges', for these show exactly what is the level of the water in the boiler. They have to be watched carefully, for should the water level fall below the top of the box in which the fire lies, there would be a good chance of the boiler blowing up! It could not blow up because of pressure alone, however, for above the boiler you can see the safety-valves — spring-loaded valves which permit the steam to escape if the pressure rises beyond the maximum that the boiler is designed to carry.

In Great Britain the limit of boiler pressure is usually 250 lb. per square inch, in the principal express passenger locomotives, though the Southern Region 4-6-2 engines work at 280 lb., and in the United States pressures of from 300 to as much as 350 lb. have been used. In the cab one of the dials is that of the 'pressure gauge', and many are the glances that the fireman directs at it, because if the pressure drops the engine is likely to lose time. On the other hand, he wants to avoid firing too hard, as in that event too much steam would be generated, and it would simply blow off to waste through the safety-valves.

As you watch the fireman hard at work, shifting perhaps four or five tons of coal in the course of a run of 200 to 250 miles, you may wonder how an American fireman manages to cope with the vast appetite of one of the vast U.S.A. locomotives of which we were thinking in the last chapter. The answer is that firing engines of such size by hand would be impossible. They are therefore fitted with 'automatic stokers', which bring the coal, broken small for the purpose, forward from the tender by long feed screws, and deposit it on the fire. All that the fireman has to do is to control the rate at which the coal is fed, a far less onerous task than firing by hand.

Well, our journey has been proceeding rapidly. The driver, we notice, has been making constant adjustments of his two main controls — the regulator and the valve-motion (or

Beginning of a test run from King's Cross. In the dynamometer car, coupled next the tender, a diagram will be drawn, by a pen connected with the coupling, showing the pull exerted by the engine on the train. This photograph was taken during the 1948 locomotive exchanges.

Inside the dynamometer car. In the foreground is the long paper roll, kept moving slowly by clockwork, on which one of the pens, seen above the handrail, draws a continuous record of the locomotive's pull; other pens record additional data.

reversing gear, as it is often called) — according to whether we are pulling hard uphill, or travelling more easily in the level, or running downhill, perhaps with steam off. All the time his steady gaze has seldom wandered for more than a moment or two away from his front window, through which the all-important signals are seen; at times he has depended on his fireman for the observation of signals seen more easily from the fireman's side, and a call or a cheery wave from the latter has indicated that all is well.

Pages might be written about the sensations on the footplate, the roar and the rattle; the incredible thrill of dashing through a tunnel, with all the noise enormously intensified, and the light of the fire playing on the clouds of steam that swirl through the black darkness past the cab; the scream of the whistle as the locomotive cuts like an arrow through all the switches and crossings of a big junction; it is all exciting beyond description to those who are privileged to travel on the footplate for the first time.

The firing slackens and finally ceases; we want just enough steam now to get us into the terminus, and no more. The driver closes the regulator for the last time, and we drift towards the arrival platform at the terminus, rolling quietly up the long platform, and stopping finally a yard or so away from the buffers that bring the track to an end. The driver looks at his watch, as he has been doing at intervals throughout the trip; and if we have had a good trip, with not too much in the way of delays, we may be sure that the result of that scrutiny is — 'on time'.

71

CHAPTER 6

Rivals of steam

THERE are countries in the world, with very many miles of railway, in which the steam locomotive is gradually disappearing from view. In some of them indeed, you might make quite lengthy journeys without hearing the familiar puffing of a steam engine anywhere. The fact is that today, a century-and-a-quarter after the first public railway was opened for traffic, steam is having a very hard fight for existence, and in many directions, a losing fight. If you go to Switzerland, for example, unless you happen to travel over one or two isolated branch lines, you may be certain to find an electric locomotive at the head of your train, or a smart electric motor-coach provided for your use.

If you cross the Atlantic to the United States and land at New York, electricity again will haul you out of the city, but before you have gone very far, in all probability your electric

The latest addition to the electric services round London is that of the Eastern Region from Liverpool Street to Shenfield, 20¼ miles. As compared with the old, cramped and slow steam trains, it has simply revolutionized passenger transport to and from the Eastern suburbs. There have been very considerable accelerations, for these trains can easily reach 70 m.p.h. and more. New electric signalling made possible a much more frequent train service.

Britain's first
diesel-electric main line locomotives

Nos. 10000 and 10001 were built originally for the London Midland & Scottish Railway. Each unit measures 61 feet overall, weighs 121½ tons, and is rated at 1,600 horse-power. In tandem, the two units together, with multiple unit control, have worked the 'Royal Scot' express non-stop between Euston and Glasgow, 401½ miles, and singly they have worked express trains of up to 15 coaches between Euston and Crewe, as well as fast freight trains. They have now been transferred to the Southern Region, where, in company with S.R. diesel-electric units Nos. 10201 and 10202, they run express trains between Waterloo and Exeter and Waterloo and Bournemouth. The latter are each of 1,750 horse-power and the 2–6–6–2 (1–Co–Co–1) wheel arrangement, whereas Nos. 10000 and 10001 are of the 0–6–6–0 (Co–Co) type.

Britain's first
gas-turbine-electric locomotive

Built in Switzerland, No. 18000 of the Western Region has the 0–6–6–0 (Co–Co) wheel arrangement, and is rated at 2,500 horse-power. The principle of working is that a fine oil spray is mixed with air which has been compressed in a turbine-type air compressor, and the mixture is ignited, the hot gases, expanding rapidly, being then used to drive the gas turbine. The major part of the power developed by the gas turbine is actually needed to drive the compressor, but there is still left the 2,500 horse-power available for traction, which drives the generator supplying current to the driving motors. No. 18000 weighs 115 tons. It is competing with a still more powerful British-built gas-turbine-electric unit, No. 18100, which is rated at 3,000 horse-power and weighs 129½ tons.

(FOR COLOUR PLATES OF ABOVE SEE OVER)

KEY TO WORKING OF GAS-TURBINE-ELECTRIC PLANT

(1) Air entry through grille at side of locomotive. (2) Turbine-type air compressor. (3) Compressed air duct to pre-heater. (4) Pre-heater, in which compressed air is heated by exhaust gases. (5) Oil fuel spray nozzle. (6) Combustion chamber, in which compressed air and fuel are mixed and fired. (7) Igniter for starting up. (8) Flame tube. (9) Gas turbine, driven by expansion of hot gases after ignition. (10) Hot exhaust gases, passing upwards between tubes of pre-heater to heat the compressed air. (11) Exhaust gases passing out to atmosphere. (A) Reduction gears through which gas turbine drives electric generator. (B) Generator, producing electric current for driving motors. (C) Electric cables to motors. (D, E, F, G) Electric motors, four in all, driving the outer axles of each bogie through reduction gears. (H-H) Driving cabs, one at each end of locomotive.

KEY TO DIESEL-ELECTRIC POWER PLANT

(1) Sixteen-cylinder diesel engine, the primary source of power. (2) Electric generator, coupled direct to the engine, and supplying electric power to driving motors and accessories. (3) Electric cables to switchboard. (4) Room housing switchboard and control apparatus. (5) Electric cables to motors of rear driving bogie. (6) Electric cables to front driving bogie, entering through pivot. (7) Electric driving motors, three to each bogie. (8) Reduction gearing to driving axles. (9) Fan and air ducts for cooling motors.

KEY TO OTHER PARTS

(10) Sandboxes. (11) Door for making connection to gangway of train corridor. (12) Driver's controls. (13) Driver's assistant (fireman) and wheel operating hand-brake. (14) Door from driving cab into engine-room. (15) Oil fuel tanks, 815 gallons capacity. (16) Engine cooling radiator. (17) Radiator fan. (18) Engine exhaust outlets and fans. (19) Sliding roof panels. (20) Grilles of engine air intakes. (21) Battery box. (22) Rear three-motor bogie. (23) Water tanks for train-heating boiler. (24) Oil-fired boiler, automatically controlled for supplying heat to train in winter. (25) Rear end driving cab. (26) Second diesel-electric unit, operated from front driving cab by multiple unit controls.

Up to the time of nationalization in 1948, the Southern Railway had not only electrified a greater mileage of its suburban lines than any other individual railway in the world, but had also extended its electrification down to the popular seaside resorts on the South Coast, which now have a wonderful service to and from London. An electric multiple-unit main line train like that shown can exceed 80 m.p.h.

locomotive, taking its current from overhead wires, will come off the train, and be replaced by a mobile power-station — two or three burly locomotives coupled together, which look like electric locomotives, but actually are diesel-electric. That is to say, electric power is produced in them by diesel engines driving generators, and this power is then used, as in an electric locomotive, to drive the train by means of electric motors. Why has steam been compelled to give way to these rivals?

The principal reason is that the steam locomotive — even of the most modern type — is relatively inefficient. Far too high a proportion of the energy produced by the coal that it burns goes to waste up the chimney, either in the form of heat from the fire, or, still worse, in the steam that it throws away. You are reminded of this when you hear a locomotive puffing hard as it starts away from a station, or works its train slowly up a steep gradient; the very noise of the 'exhaust', as it is called, is a measure of the power of the steam that might have been used to help in pulling the train, but is being lost by way of the chimney.

But as we have seen in the last chapter, the steam locomotive is dependent on the suction produced by that exhaust to provide the necessary draught for the fire. With all the improvements that have been made in locomotive design, as yet it has been found impossible to break

73

Hitherto, overhead current conduction on electric railways has been confined chiefly to main lines using alternating current at high voltage, but as the overhead method of transmission is cheaper to install than the third rail or fourth rail, it is now being installed also on suburban lines using direct current. The junction shown is Stratford, on the Eastern Region Liverpool Street–Shenfield electrification, which uses 1,500 volts D.C.

away from this inefficient means of making draught, and at the same time to mount a rapidly-steaming boiler on a chassis within a compass small enough for the engine to get through the bridges and the tunnels. For this reason, the railways have looked round for other and more efficient means of working their trains; and they have found them.

Away back in 1880 two brothers named Traill formed a company in Northern Ireland which obtained powers from Parliament to build a six-mile tramway from Portrush, on the Antrim coast, to Bushmills, near the famous Giant's Causeway. For the first time in Great Britain, they intended to use electricity for the working of their trams; a still more daring idea was that they were going to use the water of a small neighbouring waterfall to drive the dynamo that would provide them with current. Two years later the first part of the electric tramway was opened. At first, owing to the difficulty of getting powers for using the water at the waterfall, a steam engine at Portrush was used to generate electricity; soon afterwards, however, the primitive water-powered plant had come into service — one of the world's first 'hydro-electric' stations. The tramway from Portrush to Bushmills made a very shaky start, and there were many failures and interruptions of service; but it *was* a start.

The next development was of much greater importance. It was the plan to tunnel under the River Thames for a deep level railway — London's first tube — which would carry passengers from the Monument in the City to Southwark, and, by a later extension, to Stockwell. London already had its smoky underground 'Inner Circle', with its branches, but this was only just below the street level, and came frequently to the surface, so that steam locomotives could still be used. But at the deep level intended for the new railway, train crews and passengers might well be choked with smoke if the use of steam were attempted. The first plan was to use moving cables to work the trains, but eventually it was decided to substitute electricity. So with the opening in 1890 of the City & South London Railway, the first electric railway came into being.

Before many years had passed, the City & South London was running its service with no more than two minutes between train and train — something far more frequent than had ever been tried with steam up to that date. In this way, one of the great advantages of electric traction came into the limelight — the fact that with electric motors, trains can accelerate far more rapidly from rest than they can with steam locomotives. This meant that more trains could be packed on the line than ever before, and that, in suburban areas, with stations close together and many stops, a faster and more frequent service could be given — and without necessarily having to lay down additional tracks for the purpose — than with steam.

Additional tube railways were soon being driven under London — the Waterloo & City in 1898, for example, and then the so-called 'Twopenny Tube' (because of the uniform price of twopence for any distance that was charged on its opening) from the Bank to Shepherd's Bush in 1900. By 1905 the smoke-laden atmosphere of the Inner Circle had been cleared by the

Fourth-rail electrification, with separate pick-up and return rails for the current, is the most expensive form of installation, and makes for very complicated track work at junctions. But this method opposes a minimum of resistance to the current, and so makes for economy in current consumption. It is standard on the lines of London Transport, here seen west of Acton Central. The current is 600 volts D.C.

Over 400 miles of the 3 ft. 6 in. gauge main line of the South African Railways, climbing by long and steep gradients from the Natal port of Durban to the high interior plateau of South Africa, have been electrified. This mail train, from Durban to Pietermaritzburg, is using direct current at 3,000 volts, with overhead conductors. In Switzerland and Sweden, also with overhead conduction, the railways use alternating current at 15,000 and 16,000 volts respectively.

substitution of steam for electric trains. Such were the first beginnings of London's great underground electric system.

By now London's vast suburban railway network in the open air was being electrified also; and in course of time the tubes were projected up to the surface at points like Queen's Park, Highgate, and elsewhere, and the diminutive tube trains could be seen running alongside suburban trains of more normal dimensions. Railways serving the suburbs of other great British cities, like Liverpool, Manchester and Newcastle, also benefited by electrification.

With electric working of suburban trains, another valuable advantage came to light. No separate locomotives were needed. Electric motors could be attached to the axles of the coaches; control gear could be packed into a small compartment at one end of a motor-coach (in the latest tube coaches it is actually under the floor, so that it takes up no seating space at all); locomotive and coaches thus could be rolled into one in a compact unit of three or four vehicles, all of which was seating space. Such trains were economical to run, as they could be worked by a driver only, and needed no fireman.

Moreover, if more seating space were needed, as during the morning and evening 'rush' hours, two of these units could be coupled together, and by carrying the controls of the motors

The 'Enterprise' express of the Great Northern Railway of Ireland, non-stop over the $112\frac{1}{2}$ miles between Dublin and Belfast in $2\frac{1}{4}$ hours. Propulsion is by four 125 h.p. diesel engines, giving 500 h.p. in all, and this is sufficient for a speed of just over 72 m.p.h. on level track. A simple mechanical transmission is used, and the unit thus has been relatively cheap to build, as well as being very economical in running.

A new type of diesel railcar, with hydraulic transmission, is becoming very popular in the United States, as it is economical in oil consumption, and can be manned by a driver and a conductor only. Each car is 85 ft. long, and can seat up to 90 passengers. These two railcars are being operated by the Santa Fe R.R., with one crew and multiple-unit control, along the Pacific coast between Los Angeles and San Diego.

through from one end of the combined train to the other, all the motive power of the train could be brought within the control of the man at the head end. Thus, 'multiple-unit' working, by which a single driver, in effect, can drive two or three trains at once, was brought into being. This is the normal method for suburban services.

On main lines independent locomotives are preferred, so that they may be able to haul trains made up of any kind of rolling stock, passenger or freight. Electrification of a railway is an extremely costly business; on suburban lines, as we have seen, it is justified by the denseness of the traffic, but for main line electrification other reasons must be sought. In a country like Switzerland, to which I have referred already, there is one most adequate reason, but it needed the cutting off of coal supplies during the first world war before the Swiss came to a full realization why it would pay them to electrify their railways.

Go and have a look at one of the streams that come rushing down Swiss mountain valleys, and you will see what it was. That rushing water represents power, and in the Alps, with their perpetual mantle of snow and ice, it is power which can be depended on permanently, for the snow and ice melt and pour down through the valleys to feed the great rivers. Today, at a number of different points high up in the mountains, massive barrages or dams impound deep lakes of water, some of them miles in length; from these dams great pipelines are carried down the steep mountain slopes to power stations anything from 2,000 feet to more than 5,500 feet below; and here the water, under the pressure of this tremendous 'head', drives powerful turbines, which in their turn drive the electric generators to which they are coupled.

In this way almost unlimited supplies of electric current are generated, sufficient to serve the whole of the railways, the industries, and many other useful purposes. Such resources are of incalculable value in the Alps, where the working of heavy trains up long and very steep gradients has always been a power problem. In France, Austria, and other countries that border the Alps, many railways similarly have been electrified; and the same thing has taken place in Sweden.

On most of the long-distance main lines that have been electrified, the current is drawn from overhead wires, and is alternating current, or 'A.C.', at a very high voltage — anything from 11,000 to 15,000 volts — which has to be transformed to direct current on the locomotives. This is why so much more space is needed on the locomotives for all the electrical equipment than on the motor-coaches of the suburban multiple-unit trains. These use direct current, or 'D.C.', sometimes picked up from a third rail at the side of the track, as on the London Underground lines, when it is at about 600 volts; or from overhead conductors, as between Liverpool Street and Shenfield, when the current is boosted up to 1,500 volts.

In countries like Great Britain, which have not the same water power on which to count as have the Alpine countries, steam, produced from coal, has to be depended on to generate the major proportion of the current. But in a big power-station, where there is any amount of space, far more efficient means can be developed in the use of the coal than are possible in a steam locomotive.

We now come to steam's second competitor, the internal combustion engine; this entered

The 'Super-Chief' of the Atchison, Topeka & Santa Fe Railroad, on the first stage of its 2,226-mile run from Los Angeles to Chicago. It is seen climbing to the Cajon Pass in California, 3,822 ft. above the sea; later, amid the Rocky Mountains, it must surmount four summit levels from 6,762 ft. to the 7,573 ft. of Raton Tunnel. Yet the whole run is completed in 39¾ hours, at an average speed of 56 m.p.h., all intermediate stops included. The four diesel-electric units, which are worked with multiple-unit connections as a single locomotive of 6,000 h.p., are unchanged throughout.

the field at a much later date than electricity. One of the exhibits that paraded along the track between Stockton and Darlington at the historic Centenary Procession of 1925, among the line of steam locomotives, was a Ford petrol-driven bus that had had its tyred wheels changed for flanged wheels, in order that it might be tried as a passenger bus service on rails. It is hardly surprising that the success of motor cars on the roads should have suggested the use of the same kind of motive power by the railways.

Not long after this the great French motor car building firms whose names have been associated so prominently with racing cars — Rénault, Bugatti, Micheline and others — were beginning to build capacious petrol-driven railcars which were soon to be seen racing over the main lines of France, between Paris and Le Havre, Paris and the seaside resort of Deauville, and elsewhere. But petrol is a very expensive type of fuel to use for running trains; and it was another form of internal combustion engine — the diesel — that was destined to prove an even more serious rival to the steam locomotive than anything driven by electricity alone.

Diesel power had been tried on railways in the United States and Canada as far back as 1925, but it was not until the early 1930's that the first strong impetus was given to diesel locomotive building by a striking development in Germany. It was the introduction in 1932 of the celebrated 'Flying Hamburger'. Booked to run from Berlin to Hamburg, 178 miles apart, non-stop at a speed which was soon raised to 77 miles an hour average, this flyer was probably the first train in the world required to travel at up to 100 miles an hour in order to keep time.

It consisted of two long cars, seating 102 passengers, and with diesel engines as their source of power. But these did not drive the train directly. As with the gears of a motor car, some form of gearing was necessary to transmit this power from the engines to the track, and it was no easy task to devise a mechanical transmission on this scale. So it was decided that the engines should drive electric generators, and that the actual propulsion of the train should be by electric motors — a much more flexible method of control. From this successful beginning there has come the amazingly rapid spread of diesel-electric traction on railways.

Before many years had elapsed, these diesel-electric streamline trains were running all over Germany, at speeds higher than ever before in that country. A number of runs appeared in the timetables at over 80 miles an hour from start to stop. But the most startling developments in this direction are those which have taken place on the other side of the Atlantic. In 1933 and 1934 the first diesel-electric streamline trains appeared in the United States — the Burlington 'Zephyr' and the Union Pacific 'City of Portland' — and took the whole country by storm.

American locomotive builders started building diesels by the hundred, not actually built into coaches, but as separate locomotives. These are mostly of 1,000 to 2,250 horsepower, and can, if necessary, be coupled together, two, three, or four at a time, so that, with multiple-unit control, the whole series of diesel units is worked by a single crew. For the heaviest duties this great electric power station on wheels may be over 200 feet in length, over 400 tons in weight, and able to put out a total of 6,000 to 6,750 horsepower.

The craze for diesels in the U.S.A. soon spread to shunting, then to the working of long-distance freight trains. From hundreds a year the manufacturers in time found that they had got to build thousands of diesels a year, to keep pace with the demand. In corresponding numbers, the hapless steam locomotives, some even of modern types, have been hurried to the scrap heap, and on some railways of considerable size, not a single steam locomotive remains in service today.

By the end of 1952 the total of diesel locomotive units at work on American railways had passed the 20,000 mark, and some of the biggest railways, such as the New York Central, or, across the northern frontier, the Canadian Pacific, had declared publicly that their aim was 'complete dieselization'. Never before, probably, in the railway history of any country, has there been so amazing a change of motive power in so short a time.

Many reasons could be given as to why this huge expenditure has been justified. One is that the United States has its own very large resources of oil from which to draw. A second is that diesel oil is a very cheap fuel, and that the diesel engine uses it far more efficiently than the steam engine uses its coal. A third reason is the uncomplaining way in which a diesel-electric locomotive — like an electric locomotive, but without all the expense of building great power-stations and equipping the line to carry the current — can work uncomplainingly for nearly 24 hours a day straight off if necessary.

Diesels are expensive; but the mass-production methods of the big American builders have now been brought to such perfection that a diesel has come down to little more than twice

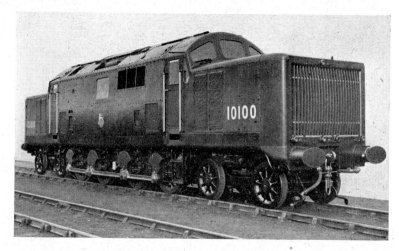

Diesel 4-8-4 locomotive No. 10100, London Midland Region. Rated at 2,000 h.p., it is the most powerful diesel yet built with a mechanical transmission, but is still in the experimental category.

The two London Midland express passenger diesels, Nos. 10001 and 10000, working in tandem, leaving Euston with the 'Royal Scot'. Together they are rated at 3,200 h.p. They are now working on the Southern Region.

the price of a steam locomotive of comparable power. And that signifies little, seeing that the diesel, with its ability to go on working continuously and (like its 'straight' electric rival) to start rapidly from rest and to put out a very big effort uphill, is worth, on the average, two of the 'steamers' that it replaces. It is lighter on the track than a steam locomotive of equal power; indeed, some railways have saved all the cost that otherwise they would have had to face in strengthening track and bridges to carry heavier steam locomotives by buying diesels instead.

So the steam locomotive is disappearing rapidly from American railways. Why are we not seeing more of diesel power in Great Britain? Well, first, because we have no oil resources of our own, whereas we have abundant supplies of coal for steam-raising. In the second place, although diesels have come into use extensively for shunting in this country, where some of their greatest advantages can be realized, the few that have been built for main line passenger service — like Nos. 10000 and 10001 of the London Midland Region — have been very expensive, and, up to the present time, there has been no standardization of diesel design, which would permit cheaper mass production.

One development here, which might alter the building cost considerably if it proves successful, has been the building of 4-8-4 diesel locomotive No. 10100, in which the problem has been tackled of designing a transmission of power in which electricity is not used. Of any diesel-electric locomotive plant, very much of the cost goes in electric generator, motors, and other equipment, but a great part of this could be saved if some form of mechanical transmission

should prove effective and reliable in the long run.

And now a third rival has come on the scene with the gas-turbine-electric locomotive, of which the first examples in this country are Nos. 18000 and 18100 of the Western Region. In these machines the principle of driving is rather like that of a 'turbo-prop' aeroplane; a turbine, turned by a stream of intensely heated burning gas and air, drives a shaft which turns an electric generator supplying current to electric motors. No. 18100 has shown herself capable of

The shape of things to come. Britain's first gas-turbine-electric locomotive, No. 18000, passing Reading with a Western Region express. This 2,500 h.p. unit was built in Switzerland, and a more powerful 3,000 h.p. British-built unit, No. 18100, also is at work on the W.R.

doing far harder work than one of the 'King' class steam locomotives, especially uphill, but as yet we have little information as to the cost of running her, or how her turbines will stand up to their work over a long period. So the motive power position on railways today is extremely interesting, and no one can say for certain in which direction the maximum future development is likely to take place.

The most substantial progress in gas-turbine-electric traction has been made by the Union Pacific R.R., U.S.A., which now has twenty powerful 4,000 h.p. units at work. Here one of them is seen hauling a heavy freight train through the mountains between Green River and Ogden, Utah.

CHAPTER 7

Railways underground

From the earliest days of railways, it has always been a problem to know how best to handle railway traffic in cities and large towns. In the United States, where crossings of railways and roads are far more generally on the level than by overbridge or underbridge, in the pioneering days it was unusual to lift a railway on to a viaduct or embankment, or to drop it into a cutting or tunnel, when it reached a town. In many towns the railway was treated as a tramway, and ran up the main street to some central depot. Even today the sight of a full-size train making its way through city streets can still be seen in the United States, in some cases in cities of considerable size.

This is a procedure, however, which we should never have tolerated in Great Britain. There are one or two towns, such as Hull, where the railways make their way into the centre on the level, which means the nuisance and obstruction of level crossings over busy streets, but in general such approaches are above street level, on viaducts, or below street level, in cuttings with numerous bridges, or in tunnels.

The same problem, in even greater degree, arose when it was realized that, with the growth of cities, railways were needed to provide quicker communication between different areas of a city than was possible when all transport on the roads was with horses. The Americans tried to solve the problem with overhead railways, carried along busy streets on steel viaducts, with their supports straddling the width of the street. One such line still survives in this country in the Liverpool Overhead Railway, carried along the Liverpool waterfront on a viaduct from

Modern tube stock of London Transport is a marvel of compactness. Many of the tube tunnels were built to an internal diameter of 12 ft., to keep the cost of boring at a minimum, and into this very limited space the trains must fit. In the latest motor coaches, all the electrical equipment is installed below the coach floors, so that the full length of the coach, save only the driver's compartment, is available for seating.

London's original 'Inner Circle', built by the Metropolitan and Metropolitan District Railways, was not tunnelled, in the ordinary sense; cuttings were excavated, partly along the centres of streets (as the Euston Road), and were then roofed over. At many points the 'Circle' comes out into the open air. Also this part of the London Transport system, with its branches, can take full-size trains, such as this handsome Metadyne set, seen at Sloane Square.

Seaforth to Dingle. But in the heart of a city a line of this kind is an eyesore, and the constant rumble of its trains is distracting; so it has gone out of fashion.

The alternative was to drop the city trains underground. But in the earliest days of underground railways, steam was still the motive power, and so it was essential that the underground trains should come to the surface from time to time, or train crews and passengers might well be asphyxiated. London's first underground railway was the 'Inner Circle', largely constructed by making a cutting along the line of streets — the Euston and Marylebone Roads, for example — and then roofing the cuttings over and restoring the street surface. At various points the 'Circle' emerged into open cuttings, and every effort was made to ventilate the remainder of the line, but older readers doubtless will remember the choking atmosphere at such stations as Gower Street and Portland Road, or Euston Square and Great Portland Street, as they are now known.

In 1890, however, there came a railway development which foreshadowed a revolution in city transport by rail. It was the opening of the City & South London Railway — the first underground railway in the world to be worked by electric power. Because of the use of electricity in place of steam, the question of ventilation was largely solved, and it was no longer necessary, therefore, to bring the line to the surface at any point. Moreover, apart from the task of getting passengers down to the trains, and bringing them up to street level at the end of their journeys, it did not matter how deep down below the surface the tunnels were bored. This was a very great advantage, not merely because the City & South London had to pass beneath the

We are indebted to London Transport for having set some entirely new fashions in station architecture, breaking away from the strictly utilitarian and often dreary ideas of the past. This station building at Arnos Grove, on the Piccadilly tube, is a typical example, with its booking hall planned as a circular tower, spacious and well lighted. The plinth on which the tower stands is equally attractive in design.

River Thames, but also because the tunnels could be bored without interfering with gas, electricity and water mains, drains and sewers, and other similar conduits found below the streets. A further advantage was that, the deeper the tunnels, so much the less chance of interfering with buildings above by the vibration caused by the trains.

Such was the beginning of the great London tube system — the most highly developed

As befits a railway system using electricity as its motive power, London Transport makes the maximum possible use of electricity in illuminating its stations at night. Notice here the floodlighting of the station frontage, with its three 'Underground' emblems, and also the illuminated station name 'Wood Green' along the fascia which forms part of the station awning, all most inviting on a cold or wet evening.

A London Underground booking office, equipped with every possible device for speeding up the work. The booking clerk prints and issues a ticket by pressing one of the buttons under the machine on the right; to his left is an automatic change machine. Tickets in less demand are stored in the racks above.

system of passenger transport by rail that is to be found anywhere in the world, and one which has been admired and studied by the traffic chiefs of all the world's greatest cities. The rapidity with which it extended has been due in part to the ingenious way in which the accommodation of tube trains is compressed into a much smaller space than that of trains of the ordinary kind — a fact that you can appreciate at once when you see a diminutive tube train running alongside a main line train out in the open. Instead of a double-line main line tunnel of 25 feet diameter or so, tube tunnels are circular bores of 12 feet diameter or slightly less,

The majority of tickets issued to Underground travellers are taken by them from batteries of automatic machines, such as the five seen to the right of the booking office in this view. The sloping panel above one of these machines shows the value of the ticket, and all the stations that may be reached at that fare. Most modern ticket machines, electrically worked, give change for sixpence or a shilling as well as the ticket.

one housing each track, and the cost of tunnelling thus has been far less than it would have been if the tubes had been required to house full-size coaches.

As explained in Chapter 3, the boring of the London tubes has been greatly speeded up by the use of automatic machinery. Circular shields, rather larger in diameter than the tunnels, have been driven forward into the soil by hydraulic power, and inside them great rotary cutters have cut the soil away; then the tunnels have been built in the form of segments of cast iron or concrete assembled into a circle, and the last operation has been to 'grout' the small space between the tunnel and the surrounding earth, as the shield is withdrawn, by pumping in liquid concrete under pressure. As far as possible, in order to keep to a minimum the vibration of build-

An underground labyrinth. At any tube junction, such as that at Piccadilly Circus, shown in this sectional view, an enormous amount of tunnelling has been necessary, for passages, lifts and escalators, to provide communication between one line and the other, and with the surface.

ings above the tube lines, the latter run under the centres of streets, and this explains why there are so many sharp curves, as the lines follow bends in the streets, or turn from one street into another.

Today there are some 50 miles of deep-level twin tubes under London, and, as you are aware, at various points in the London suburbs they have been brought up into the open, in the majority of cases to link up with the surface lines of the main-line railways, and so to enable passengers from suburban areas to be carried through direct into the heart of London. In this way, tube trains are found as far out as Watford, Loughton, Epping and Uxbridge. The longest continuous tube train journey is that of 32 miles between Uxbridge and Cockfosters, by the Piccadilly line, which has 35 intermediate stops and takes a little over 80 minutes.

So dense is the train service over London's underground lines that the number of passengers carried by the London Transport Executive's trains annually over its 213 route miles of line, and the 243 miles of British Railways over which its trains work, is nearly half the total number of passengers carried in each year by British Railways. On the average, of course, the latter

are carried over longer distances. To do its task of passenger carrying, the London Transport Executive requires over 2,200 motor coaches (including a few electric locomotives) and some 1,650 trailer coaches, which are worked to very intensive rosters.

It is at the peak hours, when dwellers in the suburbs are being brought in to their work in London, and taken home again at night, that the tube train services are at their greatest density.

Over certain routes trains are working at an average distance apart of not more than *ninety seconds* — that is, forty trains to

Tube lines have been bored at a deep level, in order to be clear of electricity, gas and water mains, and to minimize the effect of vibration on buildings above. The original lifts, giving communication between the deep level and the surface, have been largely replaced by escalators.

the hour on the same line of metals; indeed, a maximum density of forty-three trains to the hour has been reached.

The tube coaches are designed quite deliberately with a considerable amount of standing

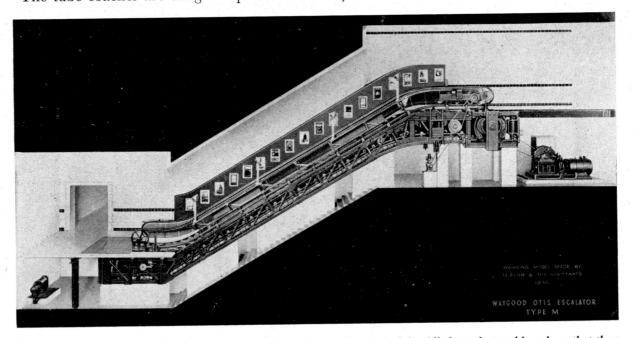

This sectional view of a tube escalator gives an idea of the working principle. All the stairs are hinged, so that they may be able to turn round a half-circle, and are mounted on an endless band, which is kept in motion by an electric motor. At the busier stations, quadruple escalators are provided, two working upwards and two downwards; or three, of which one is reversible, according to the flow of traffic.

When leaving a tube station, the driver of a train sees before him, on the left a colour-light signal, to the right a clock, and below that a headway clock showing how many minutes before the previous train started.

TRAIN RECORDING DIAGRAM

E B DISTRICT N B CITY E B CENTRAL

N B BAKERLOO E B PICCADILLY N B HAMPSTEAD

Each dial of these train recording diagrams, replicas of which may be seen at Piccadilly and St. James's Park stations, revolves once in 24 hours. The pen markings on its outer edge, made by electrical contacts set in the tracks of each tube at certain recording points, show if the train service is running at regular intervals.

space round their three pairs of double doors; were it not for the number of passengers who stand during the rush hours, it would be impossible to handle the traffic. Lengthening the trains to provide more seats would not provide the solution, partly because passengers seldom will spread themselves out to fill the ends of long trains, and partly because the increased time that would be taken in handling the longer trains at the stations would slow down the whole system.

In the working of the tubes, with trains at the density mentioned in a previous paragraph, a number of different factors play their part. One, of course, is the rapid acceleration from frequent starts made possible with electricity, exploited to the very utmost in the latest tube motor coach equipment, and, equally, special designs of brakes that can bring the trains to a stop in a minimum of space and time. On the Central London line, when it was opened in 1900, each track was sharply inclined downwards from each station, and there were corresponding up-grades into each station; the idea was to add to the electric acceleration that given by gravity in starting, and to reduce the amount of braking necessary in making each stop, but there were certain disadvantages about this plan, which was not pursued in the later lines.

A second essential in tube working is the fully automatic signalling described in Chapter 13. By means of electric track circuits, each train puts the stop signal behind it to danger immediately the signal is passed, and keeps

It is surprising, when viewing the spaciousness of the interior of a tube coach, to realize that the coach can pass through a tunnel of no more than 12 ft. internal diameter. The coach is designed with ample circulating space, especially opposite the two pairs of double doors, so that passengers may move in and out as quickly as possible, even when many are standing.

it at danger until it has cleared the next stop signal in advance; as soon as that has moved to danger, the previous signal in rear is released to clear once again. The signals work in conjunction with automatic train stops. Adjacent to each stop signal an intercepting lever is installed alongside the track, which is in the raised or 'action' position whenever the signal is at danger; should a driver attempt to pass the signal at danger, the interceptor would trip a lever beneath his motor coach, cut off his current and apply his brakes. By this system a collision on a tube is well-nigh impossible; in the whole history of London Transport there have been only one or two such casualties, and each has been due to something completely irregular for which the human element and not the signalling system has been responsible.

There is one other risk in the operation of the trains that must be guarded against, and that is the possibility of a driver being taken ill, or even dying, at his post. In this case the protection is given by an appliance which goes by the rather gruesome name of 'dead man's handle'. The controller which the driver moves to admit current to the motors of his train is fitted with a light spring, against which the palm of his hand presses all the time that the train is in motion. If this pressure should be relaxed, just as with the automatic train stop of the signalling system, the current would be cut off and the brakes applied.

An interesting detail of tube working is the 'headway clock', which at a number of stations may be seen facing the driver as he enters the tunnel. At the same moment the hand resets itself to zero, like the long second-hand of a stop-watch, and immediately begins to move round the dial once again. These clocks show the drivers exactly how far ahead of them are the next preceding trains, so that they may regulate their speed accordingly. It is wasteful of current and an unnecessary increase of wear-and-tear to hurry out of a station if the train is likely to be pulled up by a signal a few yards later.

Still more interesting are the recorders by means of which the operating authorities are able to keep an eye on the working of the entire tube system under their control. At certain points in each track on the six main tube arteries — Central, Piccadilly, Northern, City & South London, Bakerloo and District — contacts are fixed which are operated by every train that passes them. These contacts are connected by electrical circuits with the recorders, which are large dials making one complete revolution in every twenty-four hours. As each train passes the recording point, it operates the contact, completing the circuit and causing a pen to make a mark on the circumference of the appropriate dial.

The guard's controls on a tube train. The right-hand end buttons in the bottom row open and close the doors, the third button is for passengers to press themselves to open the doors, and the fourth is the starting signal to the driver. Above, right, are the buttons opening and shutting the guard's door, and left, the train heating controls. At the top is the telephone to the driver.

If the train services are working normally, the marks are equally spaced; but if a gap begins to open out, it becomes apparent immediately that something is causing a hold-up on that particular line, so that the controllers can get on to the telephone, find out what is wrong, and take the necessary steps to deal with the situation. London Transport is so justifiably proud of its services that the public is allowed to see replicas of these train service recorders in action at St. James's Park and Piccadilly tube stations.

The greatest precision in the working of the trains would be of little value, however, if the same care had not been bestowed on every detail connected with the movement of passen-

It has been possible to reduce to a minimum the platform staffs at tube stations, as well to save the passengers time and trouble in opening and shutting doors themselves, by fitting the coaches with doors that are operated pneumatically, throughout the length of the train, by the guard. At the moment of closing, the pneumatic pressure is reduced, to avoid injury to any passenger that may get caught between a pair of doors.

gers. On entering all the busier tube stations, the passenger is first confronted with a whole battery of electric ticket machines, most of which will not merely issue him a ticket in a matter of a second or two, but will give him change for sixpence or a shilling as well. Booking offices with their staffs must also be provided, of course, for those wanting tickets over longer distances or needing change for larger silver coins, but the whole business of issuing tickets has been speeded up enormously by the automatic electric machines.

With the earliest tubes it was obvious that passengers could not be expected to walk downstairs to get to their trains, some 90 feet below ground, and still less to walk up to the surface at the end of their journeys, so that lifts were provided for this purpose at all the stations. But lifts are much too slow to handle tube traffic in its present volume at the busier stations, and have long since given place to moving stairways, or 'escalators'. These provide for continuous movement, whereas the lift moves at intervals only; moreover, the passenger can speed up his journey on the escalator by walking up or down it at the same time, as many do. This is why those who do not wish the walking exercise are asked to stand on one side of the escalator, while they are being carried up or down, so that passengers in a hurry may have freedom to move up or down on the other side. Some of the escalators have been built in threes or fours, with one or two of the escalators reversible, so that according to the flow of traffic there may be two or three going up to one going down, or *vice versa*.

On the trains themselves, maximum freedom of movement is essential; hence the arrangement of the seating, with wide centre gangways and ample spaces round the double doors. Ordinary side doors to the coaches, with handles to be worked by the passengers, would be quite unthinkable; they would increase the present 20 or 25 seconds at stations to three or four times as much. So it is the general practice to have three pairs of wide double doors to each coach, which work by sliding instead of swinging, and are operated pneumatically through the length of the train by the guard. Not until all the doors are shut is the guard able to ring through the train to the driver, to give the driver the signal to start. Incidentally, though you might think it very alarming to get caught between a pair of doors as they are closing, there is no real risk; the pneumatic pressure is greatly reduced at the final moment of closing, so that you could not suffer any injury in this way. Moreover, as just mentioned, the train could not start until you were released.

No other city in the world can quite parallel the London tube system, with its small diameter tubes and the marvellous compactness of its trains. The Paris 'Metro' for the most part is a sub-surface system, rather like the London Inner Circle, with full-size trains. New York has a whole series of underground lines, serving the city and connecting under the East River with Manhattan; some of these, unlike any London tube, are 'rapid transit' lines, providing faster transport because the stops are more widely spaced and the speeds are higher. However, even London tube trains can reach their mile-a-minute speeds, and frequently do when they get out into the open country, where the stations are further apart; but that is not underground, and so is not part of the subject matter of this chapter.

In these days when the building of new surface railways has slowed down almost to a stop, and many branch lines are being abandoned, it is not the same with tube transport in the cities, and new underground lines are still being built. One under construction at the moment is at Budapest, the capital of Hungary. Even in London, with its network of tubes, finality has not yet been reached, and plans for various extensions would now have been under way were it not for shortage of money and materials since the war.

The motor bogie of a modern tube coach. The motor itself drives the axle of the nearer pair of wheels, to which it is attached, and in view of the small space available, with wheels of such small diameter as 2 ft. 7 in., it is amazingly compact. It is rated at 168 h.p., and a similar 168 h.p. motor is fitted to the bogie at the other end of the car. Current is picked up by the shoe seen at the extreme left. All the electrical control gear is equally compact, and is mounted under the car floor, instead of, as previously, taking up valuable space by being housed in a compartment of the motor coach.

CHAPTER 8

Keeping the trains moving

WHEN the 'Elizabethan' sets out from King's Cross terminus in London on its non-stop journey to Edinburgh, it is starting to make what is easily the longest regular non-stop run in the world. The English and Scottish capitals are all but 393 miles apart, and every weekday during the summer season the two 'Elizabethan' trains, northbound and southbound, have to keep moving for $6\frac{3}{4}$ hours before their journeys are complete. On the other side of the country, the 'Royal Scot' all the year round comes up from the Border City of Carlisle to Euston without stopping — one of several daily runs that are made non-stop over the 299 miles between London and Carlisle.

It is surprising that such records as these should be made within the limits of the small island in which we live. But Great Britain is very densely populated, and its people move around in such numbers that it is possible to fill a train in London with people who are all going to Scotland, and *vice versa*. If that is so, why stop the train anywhere on the way? The

A world record has been created by the 'Capitals Limited', British Railways, which daily in summer runs the 393 miles between King's Cross, London, and Edinburgh without any intermediate stop. In 1953, in honour of the Coronation of Queen Elizabeth II, the train was speeded up to cover the distance in $6\frac{3}{4}$ hours, faster than ever before, and was renamed the 'Elizabethan'. The engine is 'A4' Pacific No. 60009 *Union of South Africa*.

answer is that, the longer the run shown in the timetable, so much the more thorough must be the preparation to make it possible.

First of all, the engine must have enough to eat and to drink; if supplies run short, there will be no more steam, and the train will come to a stand. The biggest British tenders hold from 9 to 10 tons of coal, which in normal conditions is more than enough for a run of 400 miles; but water is another matter. The water tanks of the biggest British tenders hold from 4,000 to 5,000 gallons, and locomotives consume water at such a rate that all this will be turned into steam in little over 100 miles of running. But for nearly a century past the railways have been provided with means for refilling the tenders of locomotives when they are travelling at full speed.

Back in 1860, when it was desired to speed up the running of the Irish Mails between Holyhead and Euston, John Ramsbottom, Locomotive Superintendent of the then London & North Western Railway, devised a scoop arrangement by which the engines could pick up water from a long trough laid between the rails; the first of these troughs was laid at Aber, near Bangor, to make possible a non-stop run between Chester and Holyhead with the small tenders of the period. Since then, water-troughs have been laid down at 58 different points, 55 in England, and three in Scotland.

The stretch of line chosen for installing water-troughs must, of course, be level; it must also be fairly straight. Each trough is a little over a quarter-of-a-mile in length, about 18 inches across and 6 inches deep; it is filled at a number of different points from a big tank at the line side. A very sensitive ball-valve arrangement governs the level of the water, for the trough must be refilled very quickly after a locomotive has scooped a supply; otherwise the engine of the next train, perhaps 5 to 7 minutes behind, might not get enough.

Under the tender of the locomotive there is a hinged scoop, of which the business end is not unlike a large kitchen shovel in shape. As the train approaches the trough, the fireman lowers the scoop, so that the straight cutting edge is pointing forwards; the actual lowering of the scoop into the water is effected by a very slight down gradient in the rails over which the train is running. During the length of the trough, the scoop cuts off a layer of water, which the speed of the train forces, under tremendous pressure, up a curved and then vertical pipe of large diameter and through a mushroom head into the tender tank. At sixty miles an hour, a long drink of 2,500 to 3,000 gallons can be taken up in no more than 15 seconds.

A gauge on the front of the tender shows when the tank is full, and if this occurs before the end of the trough is reached, it is not an easy matter to lift the scoop out of the trough against the pressure of the water; this explains why you may have had a shower-bath when you have been travelling in the next coach to the engine, and have forgotten to shut the window while water is being picked up! For if the scoop is not raised in time, the water will come pouring over the top of the tender, and will drench the first coach or two of the train. At the end of the trough, however, a slight up gradient in the track lifts the scoop clear of the trough, and then it can be restored easily to its out-of-action position.

On the 393-mile run of the 'Elizabethan', with 5,000 gallon tenders, water can be taken

PICKING UP
WATER
AT SPEED

KEY

1. Water-softening tower.
2. Trough supply tank.
3. Pump house.
4. Pick-up troughs.
5. Coal space.
6. Ordinary water tank filler hole.
7. Air-displacement vent.
8. Mushroom head of inlet riser pipe.
9. Water space.
10. Riser pipe.
11. Hinge of scoop.
12. Scoop lowered.
13. Support bracket.
14. Counterweight.
15. Scoop lifting link.
16. Economiser lifting link.
17. Economiser guiding water into scoop.
18. Water level indicator.
19. Hand screw operating gear.
20. Engine cab.

96

from six different sets of troughs on the way; on the London Midland Region Euston–Carlisle run of 299 miles, with 4,000-gallon tenders, the troughs are more closely spaced, and there are nine different points at which water can be taken. The most curious location in Britain of a set of track-troughs is at Diggle, where the London Midland Region main line between Manchester, Huddersfield and Leeds enters the three-mile-long Standedge Tunnel by which it pierces the Pennines; the troughs are actually inside the tunnel, as this was the only level stretch to be found along the length of this very steeply graded main line. Garsdale troughs, on the Midland main line of the London Midland Region between Leeds and Carlisle, have the most lofty situation, as they are more than 1,000 feet above sea level among the Westmorland fells.

The longest non-stop runs possible without water-troughs are about 100 miles, or slightly over. The record here is held by the 'Enterprise' express of the Great Northern Railway of Ireland, which covers the $112\frac{1}{2}$ miles between Dublin and Belfast in each direction without stopping.

In England the only region of British Railways without troughs is the Southern, and this explains why the summer 'Devon Belle' Pullman has to make a stop which is not shown in the public timetables — at Wilton, just west of Salisbury — to change engines, for even the 6,000-gallon tenders of the 'Merchant Navy' Pacifics would not hold enough water for the 160-mile run between Waterloo and Sidmouth Junction.

So John Ramsbottom's invention of water pick-up apparatus in all saves hours and hours every day in the running of British trains, as compared with the slow business of drawing the engine up carefully to a water-column at the end of a platform

The vestibule connection at the rear end of one of the E.R. corridor tenders. Inside the tender, the corridor turns sharp right, and then, lighted by the circular window, proceeds under the canopy on the right side of the tender to the footplate, which is entered through a door.

CORRIDOR
TENDER

KEY

1. Sliding door.
2. Flexible connection.
3. Member of relief crew about to enter communicating corridor.
4. Communicating gangway connection.
5. Window.
6. Member of relief crew passing along tender corridor.
7. Corridor 18 in. wide on right-hand side of tender.
8. Door opening on to footplate.
9. Crew about to be relieved.
10. Flexible roof covering between tender and cab.
11. Coal space.
12. Water-tank filler hole.

and waiting there until the tender tank has been filled up. More than that, a train taking water in this way is obstructing the track on which it stands, and in this way the value of water-troughs to big junctions like Crewe and others, by enabling long-distance trains to pass through without stopping for water, is very considerable in helping to keep the platform tracks clear.

Now if you watch the engine of the 'Elizabethan' being backed down on to its train at King's Cross or Edinburgh Waverley, you will notice another piece of equipment, in this case unique, which is essential in making a non-stop run as lengthy as 393 miles. It is the gangway connection at the rear of the tender, like that at the end of a corridor coach, and the circular window on one side of it which gives light to a passage through the tender from the back end to the footplate of the engine. When the tender gangway has been connected to that of the front coach, therefore, it becomes possible, after the communicating doors have been unlocked, to walk right through from the train to the engine.

When it was first decided, in 1928, that the 'Flying Scotsman' should run non-stop between London and Edinburgh (the run now made by the 'Elizabethan'), it was realized that it was too much to ask of one engine-crew that they should work their engine without any respite for more than eight hours at a stretch. If they did not do so, however, some means had to be devised of changing the engine crew without stopping the train. The London & North Eastern Railway corridor tenders, which are the only ones of their kind in the world, were the answer of the late Sir Nigel Gresley, then Chief Mechanical Engineer of the London & North Eastern Railway, to this problem.

A compartment in the train is reserved specially for the engine crews. In this, the second crew rides comfortably until the 'Elizabethan' is half-way through its journey, and is passing Alne, 11 miles north of York. The men now leave their seats, and passing through the front guard's van and the tender corridor, a narrow space with metal walls, five feet high and eighteen inches across, they emerge through a door on to the footplate. Here they greet the driver and fireman who have worked the express from London, and after any necessary directions about the engine, the two latter enginemen retire through the corridor to the reserved compartment, to rest for the remainder of the journey.

It may be added that slightly longer runs have been made over the rival West Coast Route, between Euston and Glasgow, without the use of a corridor tender or change of crew, but on one or two special occasions only. Two of these were the amazing high speed test runs of November 16th and 17th, when the Pacific engine *Princess Elizabeth*, now No. 46201, took a seven-coach train over the $401\frac{1}{2}$ miles northbound in 5 hours $53\frac{1}{2}$ minutes, and returned the following day from Glasgow to Euston in the almost unbelievable time of 5 hours $44\frac{1}{4}$ minutes, at an average speed of exactly 70 miles an hour for the entire distance.

Actually the longest non-stop runs ever made in Great Britain followed the disastrous floods of August 1948 in Southern Scotland, when seven bridges were washed away between Berwick and Dunbar on the East Coast main line. For some time the principal King's Cross–Edinburgh trains had to be diverted from Tweedmouth by way of Kelso and Galashiels, and on several

99

On any lengthy run with a steam locomotive, an adequate supply of water is essential. The Southern Railway never laid down track-troughs for picking up water at speed, and was therefore unable to schedule such lengthy non-stop runs as its neighbours. Before the war the 'Bournemouth Limited' ran the 108 miles from Waterloo to Bournemouth non-stop, a remarkable feat for a 'Schools' 4-4-0 with a tender holding no more than 4,000 gallons. The 'Bournemouth Limited' here is seen passing Clapham Junction, hauled by No. 927 *Clifton* (now No. 30927).

occasions the then 'Capitals Limited' made this run without any actual stop — a world record non-stop distance, with a steam locomotive, of 408½ miles.

If you are visiting Paddington terminus in London, you may be intrigued to notice the starting of an express which, instead of carrying the usual red tail lamp on the back of its last coach, displays a pair of lamps encircled by discs, red and white, side by side. This is a reminder of another way in which trains have been speeded up by the cutting out of intermediate stops.

By means of what are known as 'slip' coaches, it is possible to set down passengers at an intermediate station without stopping the express to do it; though no one has thought of picking up passengers without stopping by the expedient of catapulting a coach or two out of a station on to the back of a passing express!

The principle of slipping coaches is simple enough. It requires the provision of a special slip brake coach, at the front end of which there is a special type of coupling hook. This is hinged, and in the normal running position the screw coupling of the next coach ahead lies in the cavity of the hook, the tip of which is held firmly in position by a bar which slides out of an aperture above the hook. The movement of the bar is controlled by a lever inside the

Inside the guard's compartment of a slip coach. A view ahead is obtained through the right-hand window, and immediately to the left is the lever by which the guard releases the point of the coupling hook, allowing the coupling from the next coach ahead to fall out.

Front end of modern Western Region slip coach. The coupling hook is closed; the hinged point is held in position by the sliding bar above, worked by the guard's lever. The large bell enables the guard to warn permanent way men or others of the approach of the slip.

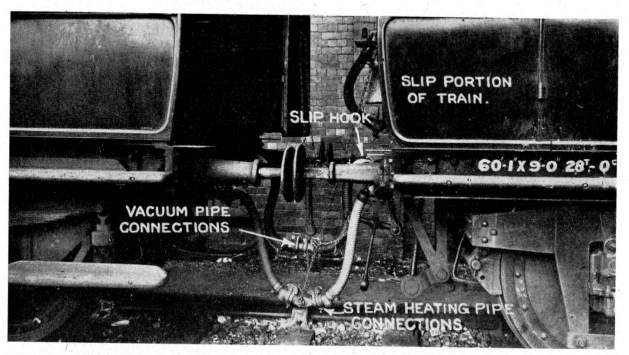

The coupling between the slip and the main train. At the moment of severance, the special vacuum pipe connection is designed to come apart without injury, and to seal the vacuum in the main train, with which it goes forward. The steam heating pipe connection comes apart similarly.

At the moment of slipping: a Western Region express from Paddington to Birmingham and Wolverhampton is just losing its rear coach, which is for Banbury, half a mile away. On the back of the slip, to the left of the gangway, can be dimly seen the special tail signal — a pair of lamps, red and white, encircled by red-and-white discs — which indicates that the last vehicle is a slip coach. Slipping is subject to very strict regulations; in foggy weather the train itself is stopped in the station to detach the slip.

guard's van. Each slip portion must carry its own guard, and he is responsible for cutting off the slip at the right moment and bringing it to rest at the station platform.

If you were riding with him in his van, you would see him start to make his preparations when the express is about a couple of miles from the station for which his coaches are destined. Part of these preparations are connected with the brake, the vacuum in which has to be 'sealed', both in the main train and in the slip portion; otherwise both halves of the train would come suddenly and violently to rest directly the train was severed.

Finally, about half-a-mile from the station, the guard applies the brakes very lightly on the wheels of the slip, and then smartly draws back his lever. This withdraws the sliding bar; the hinged top of the hook falls forward; and the released coupling of the coach ahead drops out. A special appliance carried on the flexible hose-pipe of the vacuum brake, joining coach to coach, permits the two hose-pipes to come apart without damage. Now the train is in two halves, and the light brake pressure causes the slip portion to draw well behind the express, which hurries on its journey, while the guard of the slip, with the careful use of his brake, brings his coach or coaches to rest at the station platform.

In earlier days the slipping of coaches was far more prevalent than it is today. At one time over seventy slip portions were detached from British express trains every day; several trains carried a couple of slips, while the 'Cornish Riviera Express' of the Great Western Railway slipped three times in succession, at Westbury, Taunton and Exeter, before the first stop was made at Plymouth. But the trouble of providing the specially fitted coaches, the expense of the additional guard, and the impossibility of reversing the process, to pick up passengers as well as to set them down, has resulted in the gradual withdrawal of all slipping except from ten trains on the Western Region, which has always been the scene of the greatest slipping activity.

One more device intended to speed up trains by the cutting out of intermediate stops has to do with the carriage of Her Majesty's mails. In the earlier days of British railways, mail trains were the fastest and most exclusive that were run, and it was soon realized that to stop them at every station that wanted to dispatch or receive mails would slow them down very severely. But inventive brains soon thought out a method of making all but the biggest mail exchanges by entirely automatic means.

The sorting coaches on which these mail operations are carried out are easily recognizable by the large nets that they carry, folded into a recess on the coach side; these are used to catch the mails at speed from line-side mail standards. Delivery from the sorting coaches to line-side nets is made by hanging the bags concerned from hinged traductor arms on the coach side. Delivery and receipt take place simultaneously, in an instant, as the mail train flashes past the ground postal apparatus, usually a short distance from the station serving the town concerned.

Every night two important British expresses are run carrying nothing but mails — at 8.30 p.m. from Euston to Scotland, and at 9.50 p.m. from Paddington to Penzance. The Scottish 'West Coast Postal' is the heavier, as usually it is made up to fourteen vans, at least six of which are sorting coaches; it is manned by a postal staff of nearly fifty. Much of the enormous freight of mail matter received on the train consists of unsorted letters; throughout the journey these are being sorted and tossed into great racks of pigeon-holes, according to their destinations. From time to time the pigeon-holes are emptied of their contents, which are transferred into waiting mailbags destined for the towns concerned.

One man on the train has to be more wide-awake than all his companions, if such a thing

A Royal Mail sorting van of the London Midland Region, as used on the 'West Coast Postal'. At the right-hand end is the net used for catching the pouches from the lineside apparatus, now lying folded into its recess. On both sides of each door are the traductor arms, which in action swing out horizontally, holding the pouches ready for delivery where they can be caught by the lineside ground net. To the left of the doors are the bulkhead electric lights, which light up the exchange operation. At the extreme left-hand end of the van is a 'pillar-box'.

Inside a sorting-coach of the 'West Coast Postal', with sorting in progress. To the right are the pigeon-holes, each representing a different destination, into which the sorted letters are tossed, and to the left are the mailbags, with their open mouths, into which the batches of sorted letters are transferred.

Getting ready for an exchange. A strapped leather pouch, containing mailbags for delivery, is being attached to the left-hand traductor arm; the pouch on the right is ready for delivery, with the traductor arm horizontal. The net is extended and is in the catching position.

were possible, as he is responsible for the actual exchanges, and throughout the darkness of the night must know precisely where the train is at any given moment. As the 'Postal' approaches an exchange point, if we were in the sorting coach, we should see him take the mailbags for that place, and strap them up tightly in strong leather pouches. Finally he rolls back the side door of the coach, and attaches the pouches to the catches of the traductor arms, which are standing up vertically by the van side; by the weight of the pouches these arms then drop down, against the pull of a spring, to the horizontal position, so that the pouches now are dangling well clear of the side of the train. Rolling back another door causes the folded net on the van side to leave its recess, and open out to the catching position.

Meantime a postal official of the town to which the mailbags are to be delivered has come to the lineside apparatus. He also has strapped his bags in pouches, and at a bell signal in his little cabin, which warns him of the 'Postal's' near approach, he has mounted the ground standard, attached his bags to the catches, and turned them out towards the line. As the express passes, the ground net catches the bags from the sorting carriage traductor arms, which are pulled back by their springs to their vertical out-of-action position as soon as the weight of the bags is released, while the train net scoops the pouches off the ground standard. All through the night this automatic exchanging goes on, and it is only at the bigger junctions like Rugby, Tamworth, Crewe, Preston and Carlisle, where mountains of bags are put in and out, that the course of the proud 'Postal' needs to be stayed. Not until 8.15 the following morning does the last remnant of the 'Postal' come to rest in Aberdeen after $11\frac{3}{4}$ hours of continuous running and hard work by the busy train staff.

Lineside preparation for the exchange. The postman is attaching the pouches to the catches at the top of the delivery arms of the lineside apparatus. As soon as the 'Postal' is signalled in his cabin, he swings them out toward the line, ready to be caught by the train net.

The net of the lineside apparatus, ready to receive the pouches from the train, which will be detached by the leather-bound rope across the net's mouth. The shock of the exchange is considerable, and accounts for the strength of the net and the pouches.

CHAPTER 9

Streamlining for speed

WE live in a day when one hundred miles an hour by train is no uncommon speed. It began in the early 1930's, when, as we saw in Chapter 6, the German State Railways put into service the first of their diesel-electric trains, the two-car 'Flying Hamburger', which had to be able to reach 100 miles an hour over the straight and level stretches of the Berlin–Hamburg main line to keep its schedule time. From 1935 up to the beginning of the Second World War, when the first British streamline trains — the 'Silver Jubilee', 'Coronation' and others — had taken the rails, speeds of over 100 miles an hour were reached on a number of occasions. But it is in the United States that by far the greatest strides in speed have been made. Over a number of American main lines today, with diesel-electric traction and with long and heavy trains and no mere two-car diesel streamliners, 100 miles per hour is commonplace.

A word or two first of all about the streamlining itself. Actually what is done to streamline the outside of a locomotive, so that it may cut its way more cleanly through the resisting pressure of the air, matters a good deal less than what goes on inside the locomotive. It

The Great Western Railway 4-4-0 *City of Truro,* **first locomotive in Britain to be credited with a maximum speed of over 100 m.p.h., down Wellington bank, near Taunton, with a special mail train from Plymouth to Paddington on 9th May 1904. This engine is now preserved in York Railway Museum.**

is not until speeds get really high that external streamlining has any marked effect.

When the well-known London & North Eastern Railway 'A4' streamline Pacifics were first built, in 1935, to run the 'Silver Jubilee', it was shown that at the speed of that train the streamlining ought to reduce the air-resistance by about one-tenth, and that in its turn would cut down the coal bill on this train by about 200 tons a year. Against locomotive streamlining is the fact that it covers many vital parts of the engine, and so makes inspection more difficult and repair more costly; this is why the London Midland Region has taken the streamlining off its 'Coronation' class Pacifics.

But it is what goes on inside the steam locomotive, as just mentioned, that has the most influence on the speeds that it is able to maintain. The steam generated in the boiler has to make a complicated journey before it has finished its work, and the more direct, and smooth, and easy that journey can be made, so much the better. In particular, the expanded steam has to be got quickly out of the cylinders after it has done its work, or it will make a kind of cushion behind the pistons — called 'back pressure' — which acts as a brake on the engine's efforts.

Much research has been given to the improvement of locomotive design in this way, and you may see evidence of it in such changes of appearance as double chimneys, with their double blast-pipes below, designed to let the steam escape with the utmost freedom. Your ears can detect this progress, too; first, in the explosive way in which modern engines puff when starting, and, second, in the comparative silence of their running at high speed.

Streamlining the casing of a diesel-electric or an electric locomotive, however, is as easy as streamlining a coach. It is along the side of a train, especially when a strong side-wind is blowing, that air resistance has the most effect. This is why all modern coaches have their glass windows and door-frames as nearly flush as possible with the steel coach panels. On their streamline trains before the war, the London & North Eastern Railway went even further, and fitted their coaches with flat steel 'valances' between the wheels, extending down nearly to the rails; in addition, flat rubber mats linked coach to coach, covering up the usual spaces between the coaches, so that the whole train presented one smooth surface from end to end.

What is the highest speed that can be reached on rails? Actually the highest known speed was one reached in Germany in 1931, by a specially designed car no less than 95 feet long, but carried on four wheels only, propelled, like an aeroplane, by a great petrol-driven airscrew. On a test run between Berlin and Hamburg, the propeller of this car succeeded, on a piece of straight and level track, in getting it up to the terrific speed of 143 miles an hour for six miles on end. But this vehicle was more or less a freak, and nothing has been heard of it since.

When it comes to streamline trains of the kind generally in use, it would seem that the limit to speed is set, not so much by the kind of power that is driving the train as by the air resistance of which we have been thinking. As a result, there is very little difference between the highest speeds that have been reached by diesel-electric, straight electric and steam locomotives respectively.

For diesel-electric power the Germans again hold the record; with a three-car streamline train in 1939 they reached 133 miles an hour. With straight electric power the palm goes to the Italians; in 1939 a three-car electric *rapido* reached 126 miles an hour on a test run from Florence to Milan. Steam has done a dead heat with electricity, and here we are proud to recall that the record goes to Great Britain, with the tremendous achievement of the London & North-Eastern Railway streamlined 4–6–2 locomotive *Mallard*, which hit 126 miles an hour on a special trial, in July 1938. This record was reached on the long descent from Stoke Summit towards Peterborough, on which five miles on end were reeled off at two miles a minute, and, moreover, with a seven-coach train.

But when it comes to long continuous runs at high speed, electric and diesel-electric power plants hold all the principal records. No steam locomotive could possibly have equalled the 1936 record of the American 'Denver Zephyr', which, with a couple of diesel locomotives and eight cars ran without a single stop over the 1,017 miles from Denver to Chicago — nearly as far as from London to Aberdeen *and back* — and did the entire journey in 12 hours 12½ minutes, at an average speed of 83.3 miles an hour. Some 750 miles in all were covered at 90 miles an hour. Or there is the hitherto unbeaten record of the Italian three-car electric

Leaving Princes Street Station, Edinburgh — the 'Flying Scotsman', which with an unbroken record of departure from Edinburgh and King's Cross at 10 a.m. daily since 1862 has become a world-famous train. This photograph was taken in 1928, when this express began daily to cover the 393 miles between London and Edinburgh without intermediate stop — a practice continued since the war by the relief 'Capitals Limited', renamed in 1953 the 'Elizabethan'.

On one of the fastest runs ever made in Great Britain — the trial trip of the L.N.E.R. 'Silver Jubilee' streamlined express. This remarkable vision of silver-grey and stainless steel, headed by the new 'A4' Pacific locomotive *Silver Link*, here is seen crossing Welwyn Viaduct at 90 m.p.h.; later in the journey an average speed of 100 m.p.h. was maintained for 43 miles on end, and a maximum of 112½ m.p.h. was attained twice. In normal running the 'Silver Jubilee' had to cover the 232¼ miles between Kings Cross and Darlington daily in 198 minutes, at an average of 70.4 m.p.h.

streamliner which in 1939 ran 196 miles from Florence to Milan in just over 115 minutes, at 102 miles an hour for the whole journey.

In Great Britain the highest level of speed was reached during the years just before the Second World War. From 1932 onwards there was a great speed awakening, and with the coming of Britain's first streamline train — the London & North Eastern 'Silver Jubilee' — all previous British speed records went by the board. The first trial run of this train, on September 27th, 1935, from London to Grantham and back, was an experience never likely to be forgotten by those of us who were on the train. The grey streamline engine *Silver Link*, first of her class, was only three weeks out of the shops, and no one quite knew what she might be able to do in the speed realm if she were really given her head. And she was!

At the 30th milepost out of King's Cross, between Stevenage and Hitchin, the speed first crossed the hundred-miles-an-hour line. Through Hitchin Junction the 'Silver Jubilee' swept like a hurricane at 107. A little later we were doing 112½, and for 25 miles on end the speed was continuously over the 100 miles an hour mark; indeed, it averaged 100 for 43 miles on end, and this rate of travel might have continued considerably further but for the fact that we had to slow for the curves round the banks of the Ouse at Offord.

109

The 'Golden Arrow' leaving Victoria for Dover, headed by the Pacific *Channel Packet* of the 'Merchant Navy' class, carrying its original number 21C1 (now 35001). This is regarded as an 'air-smoothed' rather than a fully streamlined design; in addition to the sheet steel deflectors on either side of the smokebox, the curious inverted trough above is designed to help in lifting the exhaust steam clear of the cab. The name of the train is stressed by the gilded arrows carried on the smokebox front, on the side of the boiler, and on every Pullman car.

This was one of the many occasions on which British locomotives have touched or exceeded 100 miles an hour. Apart from *Mallard's* unbeaten 126, and *Silver Link's* $112\frac{1}{2}$, among other London & North Eastern Pacifics *Silver Fox* has touched 113, *Dominion of Canada* $109\frac{1}{2}$ and 109 on two different runs, and *Papyrus* 108 miles an hour. Although the London & North Eastern streamliners 'Silver Jubilee', 'Coronation' and 'West Riding Limited' were limited officially to 90 miles an hour — which they had to maintain over considerable distances on every run in order to keep time — every now and again a driver would take some slight liberties in speed, and the recorder in the train would have the satisfaction of clocking a speed in three figures.

Schedule times over long distances, of course, have to take into account the various points where speed must be reduced for curves. Between King's Cross and Newcastle, for example, these include the very slow running necessary through such stations as Peterborough, Selby, York and Durham, as well as other speed restrictions of less severity. Speed naturally falls on the up gradients, also, although the London & North Eastern Railway streamliners could and did climb long stretches of 1 in 200 gradient at 70 miles an hour and more.

Allowing for all such hindrances, the timings of these trains were remarkable. The 'Coronation' had to run the $188\frac{1}{4}$ miles from King's Cross to York in 157 minutes, at an average for the whole distance that was only fractionally short of 72 miles an hour, and this with a nine-coach train. The 'Silver Jubilee' ran the $232\frac{1}{4}$ miles between London and Darlington non-stop both ways in 198 minutes at 70.4 miles an hour. All three London & North Eastern Railway streamliners had to cover the 27 miles from Hitchin to Huntingdon, pass-to-pass, in 19 minutes, at a flying average of over 85 miles an hour. The 'Coronation' ran daily between London and Edinburgh in six hours each way.

When the London Midland & Scottish Railway put its streamline 'Coronation Scot' on the rails between Euston and Glasgow in 1937, another test run showed that the new 'Coronation' class Pacifics also found not the slightest difficulty in getting above the three-figure line in speed. A test run with the new train produced a maximum of 114 miles an hour on the downhill stretch from Whitmore to Crewe, and as this tremendous speed was attained no more than two miles from Crewe Station, it was touch-and-go that the impetus of *Coronation* and her train had been reduced sufficiently, when we reached the sharply curved approach to the platform, to enable us to take the crossovers without leaving the track. This was another experience that those travelling in the train, myself included, are not likely to forget in a hurry!

Coming back that day we ran the 158 miles from Crewe to Euston in one minute under two hours, so maintaining an average of all but 80 miles an hour for the whole distance, from dead start to dead stop; once again we just reached 100 miles an hour, in flying down the slight gradient from Roade towards Wolverton. But the timings of the 'Coronation Scot' (6½ hours each way between London and Glasgow), did not require this train to reach anything like such speeds in ordinary service.

The first claim in history to have reached a speed of 100 miles an hour in Great Britain was

A streamlined French express of which all the coaches are carried on rubber tyres. Each carriage bogie has ten wheels, and the tyres are encased in sheaths which provide the necessary flanges and keep the wheels running truly on the track. Inside the train the running is almost completely silent. At first working between Paris, Nancy and Strasbourg, the train has now been transferred to the Paris-Belfort-Basle run. The locomotive is a semi-streamlined 4-6-0 of the Eastern Region, French National Railways.

by the Great Western Railway, in 1904. A special was being run in May 1904 from Plymouth to Paddington with mails off a Transatlantic steamer, and a recorder on the train maintained that the 4–4–0 engine *City of Truro* had whipped her five-car train up to 102 miles an hour when dropping down the steep Wellington incline towards Taunton. On the strength of this record the engine went eventually into the Railway Museum at York; but a critical examination of the figures since has shown that the top speed was unlikely to have been more than 97 miles an hour.

There is one well-authenticated record, however, of a Great Western Railway 4–6–0 'Castle' class engine — *Builth Castle* — having reached exactly 100 miles an hour on the way from Paddington to Worcester, down the steep bank past Honeybourne. A much more notable achievement was that of June 1932, when *Tregenna Castle* worked the famous 'Cheltenham Flyer' over the $77\frac{1}{4}$ miles from Swindon to Paddington in $56\frac{3}{4}$ minutes, covering 70 miles of almost dead level line at an average of $87\frac{1}{2}$ miles an hour. Until the war, this express was timed to come up from Swindon every day in no more than 65 minutes — 71.4 miles an hour from start to stop, booked time.

There is no record of any Southern locomotive having reached 100 miles an hour, though there is not the slightest doubt that one of the 'Merchant Navy' Pacifics could do so with very little difficulty if a really high speed were aimed at. The highest known speed of one of these

Fastest train in the world over the distance covered is the 'Mistral', French National Railways, which reels off the $317\frac{1}{2}$ miles between Paris and Lyons in 4 hours 10 minutes, at an average speed of 76.2 m.p.h. Electric power is used throughout, and the powerful 4-8-4 (2-Do-2) locomotives employed are capable of covering long stretches of line at a speed of 90 m.p.h. continuously, even with heavy trains of 600 tons weight. The second and third coaches from the locomotive are Pullman cars, and they are followed by a restaurant car.

The handsome 'Powhatan Arrow' streamliner of the Norfolk & Western R.R. skirting the New River, Virginia, on its 15½-hour journey between Cincinnati and Norfolk, Virginia. The heavy gradients through the Allegheny Mountains do not permit the high speeds attained on some American runs. The Norfolk & Western is the only large American railway which still sticks exclusively to steam power, and the 'J' class 4-8-4 locomotive shown is one of the most economical in existence.

engines to date has been 96 miles an hour. Unfortunately British railway speed since the war has declined sadly from the pre-war level; in post-war conditions there was a shortage of labour and materials, and this meant engines and track below par, not to mention the poor quality of coal and other difficulties. But the summer timetables of 1953 showed a very substantial recovery to not far short of pre-war speeds, including a number of runs booked at over 60 miles an hour.

On the mainland of Europe, also, things are brightening up considerably. The French in particular, with a terrible amount of war damage to make good, have made amazing strides in the recovery of their railways. Electrification has been extended; to the electrified lines from Paris to the Spanish frontier, by way of both Bordeaux and Toulouse, there has now been added the busy Paris–Marseilles main line, as far as Lyons, and over this some astonishing speeds are being made. Two heavy expresses daily, one called the 'Mistral', are booked to cover the 195 miles from the Gare de Lyon in Paris to Dijon in no more than 152 minutes, at a speed of no less than 77 miles an hour, and the timing in the reverse direction is all but as fast.

Practically all the long distance trains over this stretch of line, almost exactly equal in length to the distance between London and Liverpool or Leeds, now are timed at over a mile-a-minute throughout; and much the same conditions obtain between Paris and Bordeaux. On the Bordeaux route, the famous 'Sud Express' is now running non-stop daily over the

Running along the Pacific coast between Los Angeles and San Francisco is the 'Daylight' of the Southern Pacific, always filled to capacity and one of the best-paying trains in the world. The 4-8-4 locomotive and train are painted in dark red, with an orange band; the circular smokebox front is painted aluminium colour and there are bright bands across the steel fender that replaces the old cowcatcher.

360 miles between Paris (Austerlitz) and Bordeaux (St. Jean) in 5 hours, 10 minutes at 69.7 miles an hour average, and except in summer, when the British 'Elizabethan' is running non-stop between London and Edinburgh, this is now the longest regular non-stop run in the world. Even on the Italian State Railways, which also have had to do a vast job of post-war reconstruction, the first 70 miles an hour schedules, with electric power, have reappeared in the timetables.

But it is the railways of the United States that are leading the whole world in speed today. Powerful diesel-electric locomotives have taken over the working of all the principal passenger trains, and speeds are being maintained over many main lines at a level undreamed of in Great Britain. Streamline trains like the 'Twin Cities Zephyrs' of the Burlington cover the 427 miles between Chicago and St. Paul ($25\frac{1}{2}$ miles further than from Euston to Glasgow), twice daily in each direction in $6\frac{1}{4}$ hours, and include eight intermediate stops in each journey as well.

The 'City of Denver' whirls its passengers from the capital of Colorado to Chicago, 1,049 miles, in just over 16 hours every night; and this average speed of over 65 miles an hour includes no fewer than seventeen regular stops, about one every sixty miles. Recently I was shown a 'log'

One of the most famous trains in the world is the 'Twentieth Century Limited' of the New York Central System. It leaves New York at 6.0 p.m., and is into Chicago, 958 miles away, at 9.0 the following morning; allowing for the change from Eastern to Central time, the journey takes 16 hours. The previous fine 'Niagara' class 4-8-4 steam locomotives which hauled it have now given place to the all-conquering diesels, two of which, a 4,000-h.p. combination, are seen hauling it along the bank of the Hudson River.

At the tail of the 'Twentieth Century Limited'. The last car is the customary American observation car, with a glass-enclosed lounge at the rear. The train is limited to passengers who have paid first-class fare, plus Pullman supplement and a special service charge. It is formed entirely of single-room sleeping cars of different kinds, with twin dining cars, and several refreshment bars; it carries a large staff, including a 'train secretary'. Every day a red carpet is rolled out along the length of the platform from which the 'Century' leaves the Grand Central Station in New York.

The 'Twin Cities Zephyrs' of the Chicago, Burlington & Quincy R.R. are among the world's fastest trains, and are required to travel at up to 100 m.p.h. daily. Twice a day in each direction they cover the 427 miles between Chicago and St. Paul in 6¼ hours, including eight intermediate stops; the fastest run is from East Dubuque to Prairie du Chien, 54.6 miles, in 38 minutes, at 86.2 m.p.h. start to stop. Note the five 'Vista-Dome' coaches, with upper glass observation sections for viewing the scenery along the banks of the Mississippi River.

Typical of the long-distance luxury trains of the United States is the streamlined 'Sunset Limited' of the Southern Pacific Lines on its 42-hour journey between Los Angeles and New Orleans, by way of Phoenix, Arizona, and El Paso and San Antonio, Texas. Four complete 14-coach trains and one spare train are needed to maintain daily service, each with its own triple-unit diesel-electric locomotive of 6,000 h.p. One of the trains is seen here crossing the Rio Grande from Texas into New Mexico, just to the west of El Paso.

of this train, timed by Lord Garnock, on which seven runs were made in succession from start to stop at average speeds of from 80 to nearly 87 miles an hour. Such running meant a lightning acceleration from each stop, and speeds rising to between 90 and 100 miles an hour all the time the train was on the move. This was done with a train of 550 tons, equal in weight to about 17 British corridor coaches.

Far heavier trains in the United States are whirled along at continuous speeds of 70 to 80 miles an hour or more. The world-renowned 'Twentieth Century Limited' of the New York Central, a palatial train of sixteen or seventeen cars which may turn the scale at over 1,000 tons — twice the weight of a really heavy British express — covers the 958 miles from Chicago to New York in 16 hours; it has booked runs at over 70 miles an hour from start to stop, as, for

The 'Cessnock Express' of the New South Wales Government Railways is typical of modern railway progress in Australia, which has some fine trains. The most famous express in Australia is the 'Spirit of Progress' streamliner of the Victorian Railways, on the Melbourne–Sydney service; but it cannot run through, owing to the difference between the Victorian (5 ft. 3 in.) and New South Wales (4 ft. 8½ in.) gauges.

example, from Toledo to Elkhart, 133 miles, in 108 minutes. Latest figures show that no fewer than 229 trains are booked every day in the United States to make runs at over 70 miles an hour from start to stop, and the distance they cover in doing so is not far short of 17,000 miles.

When it comes to mile-a-minute runs, those in the United States reach the astronomical total of over 152,000 miles daily, 2,764 of them all told. Even in the greatest days of British railway speed, before the war, we had not got beyond 112 daily mile-a-minute runs, totalling just over 12,000 miles, of which no more than four were at 70 miles an hour or over. It was Germany that led the European speed race in those days, chiefly with the aid of its diesel-electric streamliners, eight of which were making runs booked at over 80 miles an hour every day, and 33 at speeds of over 75 miles an hour. But whatever post-war speed recovery there may be in Europe, it is pretty certain that we shall never stand a chance of overhauling the amazing speed developments in the United States.

CHAPTER 10

Inside the train

THE main problem of the designer of railway carriages is how to make the maximum possible number of passengers comfortable in a minimum of space. As with the locomotive, which is rigidly limited in size by the tunnels and bridges under which it has to pass, and the platforms and other lineside structures alongside which it must run, so with the coach. In Great Britain it cannot be more than 9 ft. wide, or very slightly over; its height must not exceed about 13 ft. 3 in. above rail; and 70 ft. is the limit in length—in fact, 65 ft. is now generally accepted as the maximum length to which coaches must be built. It is the curves in the track, of course, that are the principal limitation to length, for when the coach is running round a sharp curve, because it cannot bend its centre and its two ends are not central with the track, and the longer it is, so much the more do they project to one side or the other.

In other countries, as we have noticed in the case of the locomotives, the limits are more generous. In the United States, for example, where the tracks are not so closely spaced as in Great Britain, standard modern coaches are 85 ft. in length and up to 10 ft. 6 in. in width, which makes them considerably more capacious. It would doubtless surprise you, when walking through a modern American streamline train, to enter a luxurious lounge which has, at one

A British Railways restaurant car of the latest standard type. In place of the old fixed 'pews', the seating is in loose chairs, which greatly assist in the work of keeping the car scrupulously clean; the smooth wall and ceiling surfaces are both handsome in appearance and easy to keep clean. Tasteful shades for curtains and carpets, and ample and well-diffused lighting all add to the attraction of these beautiful cars. The kitchen and pantry car is a separate 48-ton vehicle; cooking in the latest cars is on an anthracite stove, with electric assistance.

Much provision is being made in modern trains of buffet accommodation, for those who do not wish to take full dining-car meals. In this American example, on the Pennsylvania R.R. 'Congressional', passengers are taking their meals at the lunch counter of a 'coffee shop'. An electronic 'Radarange', to the right, cooks whole meals to perfection in a matter of minutes, and an electric food table keeps prepared food hot at the proper temperature and humidity.

end of it, a stairway going upwards. You would find that it leads to an upper deck, glazed on both sides and above, with rows of seats which give you a magnificent view ahead, over the top of the train. This is specially attractive if you happen to be passing through mountain scenery. 'Astra-dome' or 'Vista-dome' cars, as they are called, are becoming increasingly popular in the U.S.A.; there is room for a lounge underneath the upper deck, as well as for the seating at both ends of the car, so that no space is wasted.

In order to increase the seating of suburban trains on busy routes, such as those of the Long Island Rail Road out of New York, many double-deck cars have been built; double-deck stock is similarly in use on some of the Paris suburban services, because the French also have ample room inside their loading gauge to build coaches of this kind in which the passenger seating space is not unduly cramped. An attempt was made to do the same thing, just before nationalization, by the Southern Railway, which had a tremendously difficult problem in handling the vast numbers of passengers who use its electric suburban services, and one or two very ingeniously arranged double-deck trains were built. But the passenger space is insufficient for comfort, within the British loading gauge, and no more trains of this type are to be built.

Generally speaking, with every increase in comfort, the weight of a coach increases in relation to the number of passengers that it can carry. Ten-compartment non-corridor coaches have

been built to seat 120 passengers, six-a-side, with a coach weight of 30 tons; this means, if every seat is taken, a quarter-of-a-ton of coach weight for every passenger.

At the other end of the scale we have the first-class sleeping car, weighing from 37 to 42 tons or so, and with ten to twelve sleeping berth rooms only, that is, $3\frac{1}{2}$ tons of coach for every passenger sleeping in it. It is small wonder that single room sleeping car accommodation is

A standard main-line corridor coach of British Railways, with four first-class and three third-class compartments. Hanging down at the left-hand end can be seen the Buckeye automatic coupler; it swings up to a horizontal position for coupling to the next coach. This method of coupling, with the bow end to the coach, shortens the connecting gangway; it also tends to reduce lateral oscillation at speed.

so expensive! It must be, or the loss in operating such vehicles would be very considerable.

External cleaning is essential if trains are to keep an attractive appearance. This carriage washing plant of the Southern Region is located near Clapham Junction. As the train is pulled very slowly through it, a series of vertical brushes, arranged cylindrically, is set rapidly rotating, and with the help of the water spray cleans the coach-sides. The time and labour saved, as compared with the old hand-washing, is considerable.

A London tube train

In its design, the modern tube train of London Transport is a marvel of compression. It has to pass through tunnels of no more than 12 feet diameter, a measurement which was chosen in order to economise as far as possible in the cost of boring the tubes. The tube coaches must therefore be built to a height considerably less than that of standard main line stock, and to a curved profile, so that the maximum use may be made of this limited space. In all the latest tube stock, the electrical equipment of the motor coaches, which in the earlier stock was accommodated in a compartment next to the driving cab, is entirely below the coach floors, so that the entire length of the motor coach, save only the driving compartment, is available for passenger accommodation.

A hump marshalling yard

For many years past, use has been made in all the larger marshalling yards of the principle of gravity in sorting the wagons, instead of the older and slower method of pulling the wagons out to a shunting neck, and then shunting them back one by one into their respective sidings. Today there is laid in, at the reception end of the yard, a 'hump' in the main shunting track; each train, on arrival, is then pushed slowly over the top of the hump, with the wagons uncoupled into ones and twos, or 'cuts', according to their destinations. A steep gradient on the far side of the hump causes the uncoupled 'cuts' to draw rapidly away from one another, so that there is time to move the switches giving admittance to the various siding tracks between the passage of each pair of 'cuts'. In the modern mechanised yard illustrated, electricity has been brought into service, to speed up the work, and with its help all the work of setting the switches is done automatically.

(FOR COLOUR PLATES OF ABOVE SEE OVER)

KEY TO MARSHALLING YARD OPERATION

(1) Wagons from reception sidings being pushed over hump. (2) Summit of hump. (3) Uncoupled or 'cut' wagon descending gradient of 1 in 18. (4) 'King' points, dividing hump track into two. (5) 'Queen' points, dividing two tracks into four. (6, 6, 6, 6) Electro-magnetic wagon retarders, or rail-brakes, by which the speed of entry of the wagons into the sidings is regulated. (7) Two-wagon 'cut' passing through a retarder. (8) 'Jack' points, giving entry into sidings. (9) Control tower. (10) Two operators, one feeding into the control machine the consecutive list of 'cuts' by which all points are made to move automatically between 'cut' and 'cut', and the other controlling the retarders. (11) Relay room, containing control apparatus. (12) Electric power-plant for rail-brakes, etc. (13) Bypass tracks. (14) Floodlights and loudspeakers. (15) Marshalling sidings. (16) Three-wagon 'cut' reaching its correct track. (17) Coal train being made up. (18, 18) Miscellaneous freight trains being made up. (19). Train of tank wagons being made up. (20) Ballast train being made up. (21) Train of refrigerator wagons being made up. (22) Wagon repair shops. (23) Complete train ready to pick up guard's brake. (24) Storage track for guard's brakes. (25) Tail of complete train pulling out of yard. (26) Main line.

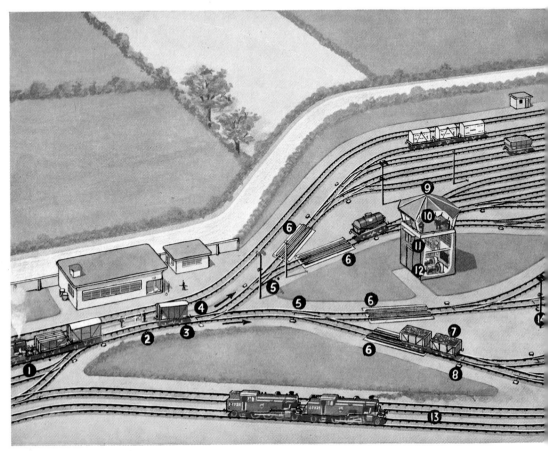

KEY TO
TUBE TRAIN CONTROLS

(1) Train-stop arm, raised when signal is at danger. (2) Trip arm on train, intercepted by train-stop, and so cutting off the current and applying the brakes should the driver attempt to pass the signal at danger. (3) Piston and spring, operated by compressed air. (4) Cables to relay box. (5) Relay box, operating signal and stop arm. (6) Red and green colour-light signal. (7) Signal number, and sign 'A' for automatic working. (8) Automatic coupling, both of cars and of control cables throughout the train. (9) Brake pressure gauge. (10) Brake handle. (11) Driver's telephone and loud-speaker to and from guard. (12) 'Deadman's handle' type of controller; if the driver raises his hand, current is cut off automatically and brakes are applied. (13) Fuses. (14) Hand-brake for use in emergency. (15) Driving cab, extending across width of coach. (16) Electric motor, driving axle through reduction gearing. (17) Shoe for picking up current from conductor rail. (18) Section through passenger seating. (19) Door-opening cylinder, operated by compressed air. (20) Throw of arm opening and shutting sliding doors, shown by dotted line. (21) Electrical equipment, all below floor level. (22) Experimental type of trailer car with roof windows. (23) Automatic signal and relays for nearer track.

With every increase that has taken place in passenger comfort, so more and more burdens have been placed on the locomotives at the head of the trains, apart from the added demands for power made by increased speeds. Corridors have taken away from the width of coaches, so that many main line coaches now seat only three passengers a-side, instead of the one-time five; lavatories and end vestibles have taken away from coach length, so that there can be only seven or eight compartments in a corridor coach, instead of nine or even ten in a non-corridor coach.

Restaurant cars are now so heavily patronized in this country that complete cars have to be reserved for eating and drinking only, and cannot be used for seating space. The latest kitchen cars, given over entirely to kitchen, pantry and accommodation for attendants, themselves weigh 48 tons. On a train like the 'Flying Scotsman', no less than

Some of the principal trains today carry decorative tail-pieces, like this gangway door on the back of the 'Flying Scotsman', as well as the name-boards mounted on the locomotive smokeboxes.

148 tons — nearly one-third of the weight of the entire train — is taken up by kitchen, first- and third-class restaurants, and a buffet car for the service of light refreshments.

For these reasons, while many express trains at the beginning of the century weighed no more than 200 tons, today weights of 500 tons or so are common, and help to explain the vast development of locomotive power that has taken place during the half-century. But 500 tons would seem a plaything to a present-day steam or electric locomotive in France, where loads of 600 to 800 or even 850 tons are met with on several important main lines. Even these loads pale before those that are coupled to diesel-electric and steam locomotives in the United States; there 1,000-ton express trains are quite common, and, moreover, are worked at tremendous speeds across the country.

Much has been done in recent years in an attempt to reduce the weight of coaches without any reduction in their comfort or smooth riding. Fifteen or twenty years ago, a massively-built American all-steel coach might weigh as much as 75, 80 or even 85 tons. But in the intervening years, with the diesel-electric locomotives, there have come in large numbers of light-weight streamline coaches, the weight of which has been cut down to 50 to 60 tons apiece — a considerable reduction. This has been done by the use of light steel alloys, or aluminium, or in other ways.

The Swiss Federal railways have done even better, in proportion; their modern 73 ft.

Observation cars at the rear end of express trains, though standard practice in the United States, are rare in Great Britain. This example works through from Waterloo to Ilfracombe at summer week-ends on the 'Devon Belle'. Before the war another Pullman observation car, the *Maid of Morven*, ran in summer over the highly scenic Glasgow-Oban line in Scotland; and the streamlined 'Coronation' of the L.N.E.R. also carried its unique beaver-tail observation saloon.

coaches, largely of aluminium construction, have been brought down from between 36 and 45 tons' weight to 28 or 29 tons, and what this means to the haulage problem over tremendously steep Alpine gradients needs no stress. In Great Britain, generally speaking, a 60 to 65 ft. main line coach weighs 31 to 33 tons; a sleeping car on eight wheels 36 to 38 tons and a twelve-wheel car 41 to 43 tons; and a kitchen restaurant car 39 to 48 tons.

Mention of eight wheels and twelve wheels in the last paragraph is a reminder of the care that has been taken in coach design to ensure that passengers shall have smooth riding even at the highest speeds. Early coaches had the axle-boxes of their wheels attached firmly to the carriage frames, and were carried on four wheels or six wheels. Some were lengthened to such an extent that they needed eight wheels for their support, in two pairs at each coach end, but these travelled very stiffly round the curves.

Then came the idea of mounting the four end wheels in a two-axle truck, or bogie, supporting the coach end through the medium of a pivot. This meant, not only that the trucks could swing and adjust themselves easily to the curves in the track, but also that the vibrations caused by slight inequalities in the track could be damped out before they reached the coach body.

Coupled with constant improvements in springing, the bogie principle has made possible

122

perfect smoothness of riding, even at the speeds of up to 90 or 100 miles per hour which are reached on some of the world's railways.

At the beginning of the century, it was popular to build dining cars, sleeping cars, and some ordinary corridor coaches also, on six-wheel instead of four-wheel bogies, as it was felt that six wheels would damp out the vibrations even more effectively. Most American main line cars also were built as twelve-wheelers. But bogie design and springing have improved to such an extent that four-wheel bogies now are customary, even for the longest vehicles. This helps to keep down coach weight, and also means that each coach has only eight wheels and axleboxes to be kept in good running order, instead of twelve.

Another interesting idea for reducing coach weight was developed by the late Sir Nigel Gresley, when he was Chief Mechanical Engineer of the London & North Eastern Railway. Having on hand some old six-wheel coaches which were in good condition, so far as the bodies were concerned, but out-of-date with their rigid wheels and uncomfortable running, he took several pairs of them off their wheels, and joined the bodies together as 'twins', putting a four-wheel bogie at each outer end, and then mounting the two inner ends together on a casting supported by a third bogie. The two coaches of each twin thus could pivot about the centre, when they came to curves in the line, and had all the advantages of smooth riding given by their bogie support.

The idea worked so well that Gresley not only rebuilt many other old coaches in the same way, as twins, triplets, quadruplets, and even quintuplets, but also began to build new rolling stock on the same principle, which is known as 'articulation'. The coaches for the famous London & North Eastern Railway streamline trains — the 'Silver Jubilee', 'Coronation', and others — were built as sets of articulated twins; many restaurant car sets were built as triplets, with kitchen car in the centre, and first- and third-class saloons at the outer ends. All London & North Eastern Railway London suburban trains also were turned out, in the first place as sets of twin vehicles, but later on as quadruplet (four coach-bodies) and quintuplet (five coach-bodies) sets.

Articulation means a substantial reduction of weight; a quintuplet set, for example, instead of being carried on ten bogies, with forty wheels, rests on six bogies only, with twenty-four wheels. There is some reduction in length, also, because it is not necessary to leave between the coach-bodies the normal space for buffers and couplings. But there is the disadvantage that it is impossible to split an articulated set into its various parts in the course of ordinary working; if one of the bogies should develop a 'hot box', for example, the whole set must be taken out of service. Little articulated stock has been built in Great Britain other than the large output of the one-time London & North Eastern Railway.

A word or two is necessary about couplings. As you may have noticed, with many coaches the ordinary method of coupling them together is by means of two links which are joined together by a screw. When the fireman or shunter drops down on to the track to couple two coaches up, he lifts the coupling of one coach, drops the hook at the far end on to the hook of the other coach, and then turns the screw until the coupling is taut, with the buffers of

Third-class passengers in Great Britain on the principal night trains between London and Scotland, now are provided with sleeping cars similar to the first-class single-room cars, but the compartments all have two beds instead of one. Otherwise all the same facilities are provided, including complete bedding, air-conditioning, individual bed lighting, and hot-and-cold washing facilities in each room. The older third-class sleepers have lying-down accommodation only, in four-berth compartments.

the two coaches just nicely touching.

But if you have watched the coupling of main line coaches on what were the London & North Eastern and Southern Railways, you will have seen a different procedure. The couplings, when disengaged, look rather like steel hands; and when the coaches are pushed together, the two hands come together in a hand-clasp that does not let go. The idea is American, and is in universal use in the United States and Canada, on wagons as well as coaches. It has considerable advantages, because the whole of a train coupled in this way is like a long jointed frame. This leads to steadiness of riding; another important point is that in the event of a collision or a derailment, as has been proved when these casualties have occurred, a train can be held in line, instead of spreading itself all over the track, and the dangerous tendency of coaches to ride over one another, or 'telescope', is largely prevented. This method of coupling is now the British Railways standard for new main line corridor coaches.

At one time there used to be three classes of coach in Great Britain — first, second and third — and some Continental countries, like Germany, even had a fourth class. But the tendency in these days is for there to be two classes only. In Great Britain, second class has disappeared, except on boat trains carrying Continental passengers, where 'seconds' are still to be found because there is still second-class travel abroad. In the United States travel is either 'first class' or 'coach'. The latter is the equivalent of third-class travel here, but on long-distance journeys today the fortunate American 'coach' passenger is carried in luxurious 'reclining chairs', which can be tilted to any angle, and are provided with armrests and footrests, so that the passenger has every chance of sleeping comfortably at night. Most American cars for day travel are open from end to end, and not of the compartment type to which we are accustomed.

North American passengers with first-class tickets usually travel 'Pullman', paying a supplement for the privilege, according to the type of accommodation that they occupy. For day use

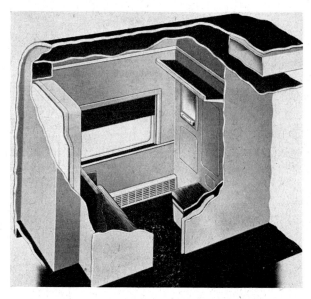

A 'roomette' compartment in an American sleeping car. In this view the compartment is arranged for day use, with its seat on the left-hand side, the bed in a vertical position behind the seat, and the washing facilities folded up into the opposite wall. A fine view is obtained through the wide window, and there is ample luggage space.

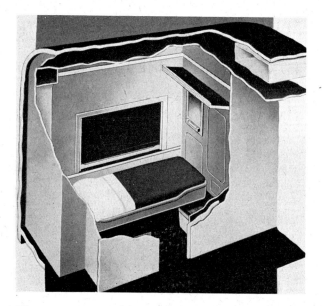

The compartment has now been transformed for the night. The seat back has been folded forward, and the bed let down on its hinge, across the full width of the compartment. In the morning, a finger touch is sufficient to swing the bed, which is balanced, back into the wall, and there is then ample space for dressing.

there are 'drawing-room cars', furnished with armchairs and all kinds of modern accessories, like the Pullman cars run in Great Britain on trains such as the 'Queen of Scots', 'Yorkshire Pullman', 'Golden Arrow', 'Devon Belle', 'Bournemouth Belle', and others. For night occupation, there are all kinds of sleeping cars. The old Pullman 'standard' sleepers have seating of the ordinary kind for day use, but are converted at night into sleeping cars by pulling the seats together to form lower berths, and letting down sections of the roof, on either side of the central gangway, to form upper berths. Mattresses, sheets and blankets are then laid in each berth, and curtains are drawn along both sides of the aisle to give a measure of privacy.

But the modern sleeping cars are all of compartment types, and some of them, like the 'roomette' cars, are of most ingenious design. Each passenger has a small and comfortable private room for day use, in which at night he undresses and prepares for bed; when he is ready, a touch on a catch in the compartment wall, and down comes the bed on a hinge, all made up and ready to sleep in. Similarly in the morning the bed, which fills most of the little room when it is in position for occupation, can be folded up into the wall when the time has come to get up and dress. In addition to roomettes, there are single bedrooms, double bedrooms, and 'master rooms', which are suites of rooms complete with a shower bath. The supplement which the passenger pays for this luxury depends on the amount of space that he occupies.

The convertible type of car is a necessity in a country like the United States, with its lengthy journeys, for to provide separate accommodation for day and night use would make the trains inordinately lengthy. A modern long-distance American express in any event is a massive formation; it probably begins with two or three 70 ft. diesel-electric locomotive units; then

One of the highly popular 'Vista-Dome' or 'Astra-Dome' cars which are now being introduced into many American long-distance train formations, especially over routes through mountain country which are noted for their scenic attraction. The ample American loading gauge makes it possible to build cars with two decks, each with ample head-room; this upper deck, glazed all round, commands magnificent views above the roofs of the coaches ahead.

A modern Pullman 'parlour car'. It forms part of the 'Congressional' of the Pennsylvania R.R., the fastest train of the day on the New York-Washington service. This car has air-conditioning, safety glass, pneumatically-operated end doors, rust-coloured upholstery to its comfortable reclining chairs, blue curtains and carpet. At the end is a separate 'drawing room' compartment with five seats. The car is in charge of the coloured 'porter' seen at the rear.

come a baggage car, a post office and 'express' (parcels) car, a lounge for 'coach' passengers (probably including dormitory accommodation for the train staff), several reclining chair cars, a 'café' or 'tavern' car, a dining car, a series of Pullman sleeping cars, with various accommodation, and, on the tail, a combined sleeping and observation car — the last with a bow window of glass at the rear end, which forms a pleasant *rendezvous* for Pullman passengers, and probably is provided also with refreshment service.

A bedroom on the 'California Zephyr'. Behind the lady's seat is one of the two beds, folded up into the wall during the daytime, and brought down to the horizontal at a touch when unlocked by the lever shown. Controls of light, heat, and ventilation are to the right of the small door that admits to the toilet.

The crews of these trains — including restaurant and refreshment car staffs, an attendant or 'porter' for each sleeper, baggage-men, the all-important conductor, sometimes a lady 'hostess', a barber and even a 'train secretary', and, of course, the enginemen — at times run to a total of thirty or more. On some of the most famous trains, like the 'Twentieth Century Limited', a special service charge is levied, in addition to first-class fare and Pullman supplement, to help in covering the cost of this army of attendants. An American train, indeed, is in every way like a hotel on wheels.

On the mainland of Europe the majority of the dining and sleeping car services are under the control of a single company — the 'Compagnie Internationale des Wagons-Lits et des Grands Express Européens', or International Sleeping Car Company. In the past this was responsible for working the *trains-de-luxe*, like the 'Blue Train', 'Orient Express', 'Simplon–Orient Express', 'Rome Express', and many others. At one time these famous flyers would not look at any travellers other than those provided with first-class sleeping car tickets, and were made up exclusively of first-class sleeping and dining accommodation; but today they have become much more democratic, and include second-class sleepers and even ordinary first- and second-class coaches. Apart from the United States, the day of 'first class only' is definitely at an end.

CHAPTER II

Stations, timetables and train running

IF you want to get a real idea of what it means to operate a railway station in the busiest possible conditions, you should visit a London terminus such as Waterloo or Liverpool Street at the height of the morning rush hour. Trains are running in, each one packed with passengers, practically every minute, and sometimes two or even three simultaneously; each train is disgorging seven hundred, eight hundred, perhaps even as many as a thousand passengers. Before the last of them have passed the ticket barriers, probably, the train that brought them has started out again.

All this is being done in perfectly orderly fashion; each train is finding its way at its appointed time to its appointed platform; occasional interruptions of the flow may cause hold-ups that soon spread well down the line. But though there are such deadly enemies of punctual working as engine failures, and, worst of all, fog, the way in which our great terminals handle their dense traffic with few lapses from punctuality is little short of marvellous. And when the evening comes, of course, all the inward rush that we saw in the morning is seen once again, but this time in reverse. The evening problem is, perhaps, the more difficult of the two, because the maximum density of traffic, generally speaking, is compressed into a shorter period of time than the morning rush.

Some of the station statistics tell their own tale. Waterloo, with its 21 platforms, reckons to handle between 1,300 and 1,400 separate train movements, in or out, every working day. Liverpool Street, with 18 platforms only, has well over 1,000 daily train movements, and in this case a relatively small proportion only are electric trains; all other trains have to detach the engines that have brought them in, and to attach fresh engines to take them out, all of which adds greatly to the complication of the signal and switch movements. The combined Victoria and Exchange stations at Manchester, with 22 platforms between them, also have a very busy day, with rather over 1,100 movements of trains, some of which run through, because the station is only partly terminal.

But all these figures pale beside those of London Bridge and Clapham Junction, the two busiest stations in Great Britain. To stand on the London end of one of the 17 platforms at Clapham Junction at the busier times of the day, and to see trains dashing past in all directions, sometimes several of them within the compass of a single minute, is a thrilling sight indeed; more than 2,000 trains pass through or stop at Clapham Junction every day. London Bridge beats even this record with rather over 2,100 trains daily, but here only six of the 21 platforms are 'through', and the few trains which do not deign to stop at London Bridge are travelling very slowly because of the curves.

It is of interest to compare Britain's biggest stations with some of those in other countries. You may have noticed how, in recent years, many large British stations have been made more cheerful by the opening of shops of various kinds, and even of news cinemas in which passengers can while away their waiting time, and the proceedings often are enlivened still further by the broadcasting of music. Some of these ideas have come to us from across the Atlantic. In general, American passengers do not wait for their trains on the platforms of their stations, but in comfortable buildings, the platforms being no more than narrow covered passages from these buildings to the trains. In some of the great cities, the stations are of almost unbelievable size and magnificence.

Let us make our way, for example, into the Grand Central Station at New York, terminus of the great New York Central

Suburban train operation requires the accommodation of the maximum number of passengers in the minimum of space. With their ample loading gauge, American railways can build double-deck suburban cars, like the Burlington type shown here, which has galleries with upper seats along both sides of the car. The upper seats are reached by the end stairways.

System. It is like walking into a cathedral, for the main entrance hall is 125 feet high, 120 feet wide and 275 feet long. Round its walls are a series of shops, and opening off it we find a cinema, an art gallery, a restaurant, and corridors leading direct to neighbouring hotels and office buildings. Through this hall and other approaches to the station there pass some fifty million passengers every year. It forms part of an above-ground structure 700 feet by 400 feet, but this is a fraction only of the station itself, which has been blasted out of the solid rock beneath the city and, so far as the trains are concerned, is entirely underground.

The 'business' part of the station is on two levels. The main-line station, with 41 tracks, is 20 feet below street level, and the suburban station, with 39 tracks, is 44 feet down. At their inner ends many platform lines of the suburban station connect with loop lines, providing a semi-circular course by which trains can be worked round direct from the arrival to the departure side of the station.

Needless to say, the operation is entirely electric; approach to the station is by means of a four-track tunnel under the length of Park Avenue. Certain of the tracks are signalled for reversible working, so that during the inward morning rush there are three tracks available for trains approaching the terminus, and one for exit, whereas in the evening outward-bound trains use three tracks, and incoming trains the fourth.

The Pennsylvania Station in New York, also entirely below ground level so far as the railway itself is concerned, is nearly as large. It differs from the Grand Central Station, however, in that it is of the 'through' type, approached by under-water tunnels from both directions.

The Pennsylvania main line comes under the Hudson River from New Jersey into Manhattan Island; and the line then continues under the East River to the great Sunnyside yards on

Exterior of the double-deck coach, showing the windows to the upper and lower decks. The coach has the corrugated stainless steel sides which are very popular now in American coach construction, because of their combination of strength with light weight. Some railways, like the Burlington, leave the attractive bright steel panels without painting.

Long Island, and to connections with both the Long Island and the New York, New Haven & Hartford Railroads. On the New York Central station and its approaches, the equivalent of £30,000,000 was spent, and on the Pennsylvania station £23,000,000; today the cost would be more than twice as great.

In many of the great American cities, the various railways serving them have combined to build one 'Union Station', which is used by all their passenger trains. Some magnificent examples of this co-operative enterprise are found in Washington, Chicago, Cleveland, Cincinnati, St. Louis, and elsewhere. The Union Station at St. Louis boasts no fewer than 42 tracks to accommodate its long-distance trains, serving all parts of the United States.

The working of a railway station is under the control of a stationmaster, and all the station staff are responsible to him — booking clerks, signalmen, porters, shunters (if the station has a goods depot), and, at the larger stations, inspectors and many other types of railwaymen. If the station is a really big one, the stationmaster, even if he no longer wears the once distinctive uniform of a frock coat and top hat, is in effect the commanding officer of an army of very considerable size. He represents both the commercial and the operating sides of the railway, and so is the channel of communication between the railway and the public, whether in connection with passenger traffic or the movement of freight.

In the early days of railways, no train was allowed to start from a station, even though all the signals had been pulled off, until the stationmaster had given the guard his authority. The rule still is in force, but at any large modern station it would be completely impossible for the stationmaster to attend personally to such details of working as this, through the day and through the night as well. So he may delegate his authority to a platform inspector, or, at a smaller station, to a foreman porter. The guard, on his part, has to make certain that the starting signal is pulled off before he gives the driver the 'right away', and the latter must not attempt to start until either he or his fireman has seen the guard's green flag waved, or, at night, his green lamp.

At the bigger stations, the stationmaster exercises his authority through platform inspectors, who are on duty in shifts both by day and night. The working of an important junction like Crewe or York is a very complicated business. Most careful arrangements have to be made as to the platforms which are to be used by each individual train, and directly any new issue of the time-tables comes out, the platform workings have to be checked in order to ensure that trains will not be held outside the station, waiting for platforms to which to run, and blocking the lines meantime. Often, if trains are running late, last-minute alterations have to be made, and here the modern 'public address' system of station loudspeakers is of the greatest value, for

'Push-and-pull' working of suburban services is planned to avoid the necessity for running the locomotive round the train at the terminus before the return journey is begun. The locomotive is therefore attached to one end of the train, and the principal controls are carried through to a driving compartment at the other end. When the engine is pushing the train, the fireman remains on the footplate, but in communication with his driver by telephone. This photograph shows a Paris suburban 'push-and-pull' train of the Nord Region of the French National Railways, with 2-8-2 locomotive.

London's finest terminus is undoubtedly Waterloo of the Southern Region. Rebuilding of the old and inconvenient Waterloo was completed in 1922, and the new station was opened by Queen Mary. A wide and spacious circulating area extends across the full width of the station, with booking and enquiry offices, post office, refreshment and dining rooms, and headquarters offices opening off it on the right. To the left are the train departure and arrival indicators, and the entrances to the 21 platforms. The platforms of the Waterloo tube stations have various approaches, including one in the centre of the circulating area.

The dense electric suburban services to and from all parts of south-west London make Waterloo the busiest of all London terminal stations. There are also the services handled by steam locomotives to the West of England and the Bournemouth lines. Every 24 hours Waterloo handles between 1,300 and 1,400 individual train movements, with the help of electric signalling. The only portion remaining of the old station is seen, in part, at the extreme left of this view, and accommodates trains for the Richmond, Windsor and Reading lines. The entire station covers 24 acres.

TELEGRAPH OFFICE
←←← PUBLIC TELEPHONE

GENERAL ENQUIRY OFFIC
RESERVED SEATS & SLEEPING BER

BOOKING OFFICE
LADIES WAITING ROOM
PUBLIC TELEPHONE
SUBURBAN STATION

Much has been done during recent years to brighten up our big terminal stations. This view of No. 10 departure platform at King's Cross, just before the departure of the 'Flying Scotsman' for Edinburgh, is typical. Note the clear projecting signs directing to the various offices, and illuminated at night; the bookstall, on the left, is one of several shops. From time to time passengers are entertained by records played over the station loudspeakers.

it enables clear announcements to be made to passengers on the platforms in any part of the station.

The previous paragraph is a reminder of the importance of the railway timetable, which marks out, in effect, the 'path' in time which is to be followed by each train. In earlier railway days the advantage was realized of setting out the train service in some way which would appeal readily to the eye, and many railways prepared large boards, each one representing a fairly lengthy section of one of their main lines, on which the 'path' of each train was represented by a coloured thread. The station names were arranged vertically up the side of the board; horizontally it was divided into hours and minutes, over the 24 hours of the day; and pins, inserted at the position of each stop made by each train, held the threads in position. The speed of a train was evident from the slope of the thread, the threads nearest to vertical in their inclination representing the fastest trains. The amount of space between any two threads indicated where it was possible to find a path for an additional train.

In the course of time this old method has given place to the large train service graphs which are now used in almost all timetable offices as the basis of timetable compilation. The threads and pins have been replaced by ink lines, and the chief advantage, of course, is that any number of copies of the graph are available, if needed, as compared with the one cumbrous and complicated board. On the continent members of the railway staff often prefer to carry in their pockets a folded copy of the *graphique*, as they call it — that is, a train service diagram of the line over which they are travelling — rather than a copy of the timetable book to which to refer for their trains.

From the train service diagrams there are prepared the printed timetable books and sta-

Most handsome of London station exteriors is that of St. Pancras, with its Gothic frontage, opened in 1868. It was built to serve as the terminus for the Midland Railway, last but one of the original British main lines to reach the capital.

tion sheets for the use of the public. Often you may think that the search for a train in a timetable is a terribly complicated business (though it is not really, if you learn to find your way about a timetable), but the complications of the public books are nothing to those of the 'working timetables' which are printed for the use of the staff. These show the times, not only of passenger trains, but also of freight trains, empty carriage trains, light engines, and various other miscellaneous workings. With express trains making few stops, the times are printed at which they are expected to pass every important junction station or other timing point, in addition to their various starting and stopping times.

Much other information is printed in the working timetables, such as the lines on which trains are booked to run (where there are four or more tracks), the junctions at which trains must switch from fast to slow tracks, and *vice versa*, the points at which slow trains are to shunt in order to enable faster trains to pass them, stops to enable locomotives to take water, and so on.

The working books are thus very considerably larger than the public books, and have to be issued in a number of sections; the Western Region working timetables, for example, are issued in 17 sections, with a total of nearly 3,000 pages.

Every week, for one reason or another, special trains have to run — duplicates of regular trains, trains for special parties, excursions, and so on — and these must also be timetabled, or they would produce chaos in the working. Weekly working notices are therefore printed, in which all the special workings are shown, with any other matters of which the operating staff needs to be informed. A companion weekly notice is issued by the engineering department, giving details of all points along the line at which repairs are being made to the track, and particularly those which require drivers to reduce speed in order to ensure safe running. These notices are issued to all members of the staff who normally receive copies of the working time-tables.

One job of extraordinary complexity is that of arranging 'diagrams' of the working of both engines and rolling stock. Engines and their crews are earning money for the railway only when they are actually pulling trains, and the time of both must therefore be used to the maximum possible advantage while the engines are in steam. Moreover, as we have seen already in Chapter 4, different classes of engine are designed for different types of work, and although we have today many engines of 'mixed traffic' types, which can be used at will on passenger or freight trains, there are other classes, like the principal express engines, which as far as

St. Pancras has the largest all-over station roof in Great Britain, with a clear span of no less than 210 feet. But its accommodation is very limited, as it has only seven platforms. The main roof ties are below the platforms, and the lower part of the station is used largely as a store for beer that has been brewed at Burton, on the one-time Midland system.

The approach to Flinders Street Station, Melbourne, one of the busiest railway stations in the world; every day it handles over 300,000 passengers. With the adjacent Princes Bridge station, it has 11 platforms, and most of the tracks run through under the central concourse from one station to the other. No. 1 platform, which is continuous through both parts of the station, is 2,097 ft. long and the longest in Australia. In the extreme top right-hand corner of this view may be seen one of the stands of the famous Melbourne Cricket Ground.

possible should be kept to fast and heavy passenger work. When a locomotive goes out from its home station, therefore, a suitable return working must be arranged, with a margin of time left between each turn of duty for attention to the fire and other locomotive requirements, and careful attention to the number of hours worked by the crew.

The working of passenger rolling stock is an even more complicated business. In general, coaches are made up into sets, and in suburban areas, where the journeys are short and the composition of the trains does not change, the diagramming is not so difficult. But with main line stock it is different. Apart from the main train set, there may be through coaches to be worked to distant destinations. Extra vehicles may need to be attached on certain days, at week-ends in particular, to cope with the rush of passengers. Some coach sets may make circular tours lasting for several days before they return to their home stations. Putting the coach diagrams together is, indeed, like a jigsaw puzzle on an enormous scale, and if you should have to stand on one of your holiday journeys, it is well to remember the magnitude of this problem, and that it is by no means easy to produce even a single coach at short notice in order to cope with an unexpected rush.

Before we finish this chapter, it is worth mentioning one responsible member of the railway

Biggest and most imposing of all railway stations in Africa is the new Central Station at Johannesburg, a city with over 500,000 inhabitants, and centre of the renowned gold-mining area known as the Rand. A dense service of electric trains links both the mining and the suburban areas round the city with this station; there are also the long-distance steam trains. All tracks are laid to the standard South African gauge of 3ft. 6 in. only. The station ultimately will have 16 platforms.

In many countries, particularly the United States, the platforms of a terminal station are not used by passengers when waiting for trains, but are regarded merely as passageways to and from the trains. All the accommodation for passengers is concentrated in one main station building, and some of these modern buildings are notable for their beauty as well as their comfort. This great concourse of the new Central Station at Johannesburg, South African Railways, with its graceful arched roof, is a magnificent example of what can be done in this direction.

137

Most amazing of all the world's railway terminals is the Grand Central Station of the New York Central System in New York City. Under the main building is a vast cavern, blasted from the solid rock, and large enough to accommodate 41 long-distance tracks, with 39 suburban tracks at a still lower level. Loop tunnels permit trains after arrival to run round to the departure side without fouling other arrivals and departures.

operating staff of whom we see a great deal on our journeys; I refer to the guard. His name, like that of the driver, comes down to us from stage-coach days. Indeed, in the earliest railway days, the guard had an unenviable position on the train closely resembling that which he occupied on a coach, sitting on a seat high up at the end of the last coach, exposed to the weather and to the engine smoke. It is very different today, for in the latest brake-vans, the guard has a small compartment to himself, with comfortably padded seat, warmed in winter, and with a periscope with enables him to see along the whole length of his train without even leaning out of the window.

The guard and the driver are jointly responsible for the safe working of their train. Among his various duties, the guard must see that his train is correctly made up and coupled up, that the brake is working properly, and that the last coach carries a tail-lamp, for reasons that are mentioned in Chapter 13. As previously mentioned, the driver is not allowed to start his train until he has received the 'right away' from the guard. The latter is in charge of all the luggage carried in his van, and for keeping a record of the running of his train, including the number of the engine, the name of the driver, all starting, stopping and passing times, and the reasons for any loss of time. If there is any breakdown of his train, the guard must take steps to protect it by walking back along the line and laying down detonators on the rails. In the normal course, the signalling described in Chapter 13 should be quite sufficient protection, but the detonators are an additional warning to any following train, should such be needed. Thus the guard of your train is a guard in reality as well as in name.

The main line concourse of the Grand Central Station has the dimensions of a cathedral; the vaulted building is 120 ft. high, 120 ft. wide, and about 250 ft. long. Round this hall shops are grouped and opening off it are a cinema, an art gallery and a restaurant. The three great windows illuminate the hall by day, and fluorescent lighting by night.

CHAPTER 12

Moving the freight

O N busy American main lines today it is becoming the fashion to provide radio communication between the engine, at the front end of a freight train, and the 'caboose'
at the back, which is the equivalent of our guard's van. And the reason? Because many
modern American freight trains are a mile or more in length! If the train crew, in the caboose,
have got to set one of their number walking that mile to the engine, in order to get a message
to the driver, and the man has then to walk back again, anything up to three-quarters-of-an-
hour may be wasted.

Hence the radio arrangements, which permit engine-crews to talk to train crews while the
train is in motion, or *vice versa*; also the men on one train can talk to the crew of another
travelling in the opposite direction, or to sending and receiving stations by the line-side.

**A typical London Midland Region freight train, drawn by a 2-8-0 locomotive, the wheel arrangement used most
extensively in British goods train working. The headlights show this to be an express freight, Class 'F', of which the
speed is limited because the continuous brake is not in use (even though some of the wagons may be fitted with it).
The only brake-power available, therefore, is that of engine, tender and guard's van.**

The fastest freight trains are those in which the wagons are fitted throughout with continuous brakes, like the passenger coaches, and these may be run at maximum speeds up to 60 m.p.h. The example seen is on the Eastern Region, British Railways, and is headed by a 2-6-2 'Green Arrow' mixed traffic type locomotive, which is equally at home on express passenger trains. It is bound for London, and is emerging from Hadley Wood tunnel.

Needless to say, this radio equipment has greatly speeded up the working of the trains.

In the United States and Canada all the wagons that make up the freight trains are long 40-foot or 50-foot 'cars', as the Americans call them, carried on eight wheels apiece. Open wagons used for coal, ore and other minerals can carry upwards of 50 tons, and sometimes up to 100 tons in a wagon.

It is nothing on a number of American main lines to marshal a hundred of these vehicles in a train. The record is probably reached by certain railways which bring iron ore down from the Mesabi Mountains of Minnesota to the docks at Duluth on Lake Superior, where the ore is transferred to the steamers that ply on the Great Lakes. These ore trains are made up regularly to 180 bogie wagons each; from the mines to the docks the load is running mostly downhill, and then the enormous steam locomotives used work the 180 empty wagons back up to the mines again. Such trains as these are fully a mile-and-a-half long.

On a test run that was made over the Chesapeake & Ohio Railroad with one of the immense 2-6-6-6 type articulated steam locomotives of that company — which with their tenders weigh 513 tons each in full running order — a train of 160 bogie wagons of coal was put together, weighing in all 14,083 U.S. tons. In British tons of 2,240 lb. this would be about 12,575 tons, and equal to at least ten British 60-wagon freight trains stretched out one after

141

Despite the limitation of a track gauge only 3 ft. 6 in. wide, the South African Railways have developed some extremely powerful locomotives, such as this articulated Beyer-Garratt example. It is of the 4-8-2-2-8-4 type, measures 94 ft. overall and weighs 175 tons; to keep the axle-loading down to 15 tons, a further 6,750 gallons of water are carried in a bogie tank wagon. The locomotive is seen working a coal train in the Rand, near Johannesburg.

the other. The vast engine got its train on the move; a mile from the start it was travelling at 19 miles per hour, and 11 minutes after starting the speed was 29 miles per hour; eventually a top speed of 46 miles per hour was reached. By then the engine was pulling on the leading wagon with a force of all but 7,500 horse-power!

A good many reasons might be given as to why it has paid the Americans to develop the working of these prodigious loads with single locomotives up to three times the weight, the size and the power of the biggest in Great Britain. One, at any rate, is the cost of labour. Another is that many main lines are single track over long distances, so that the concentration of loads means that fewer trains have to be handled. This is a great advantage in arranging the 'meets' by which the trains in opposite directions get past one another at the various passing loops.

In recent years there have been remarkable developments in the working of long stretches of single track main line in the United States. It makes all the difference, as you can well imagine, if a single control office can see what is happening at any given moment, over, say, 50 or 100 miles of line — where each train is, at what loop it will be best to hold up a train travelling in one direction so that one running the other way can get past it, and so on. This is exactly what is done with up-to-date 'centralized traffic control', or 'C.T.C.' for short. Not only has the one control office a picture of the whole section controlled, but by long-distance electric circuits it is able to work all the loop switches and signals, up to perhaps 50 miles or more away!

Lengthy loops are laid in for passing purposes, and it is nothing unusual for trains approaching one another from opposite directions on the single track to pass at reduced speed through a loop without either actually coming to a stand. So efficient has single line working become in the U.S.A., with the help of 'C.T.C.', that some double lines, not too heavily burdened with traffic, have been converted to 'C.T.C.'-equipped single lines, without any slowing down of the trains, and the cost of maintaining one of the two tracks in this way has been done away with.

Another way in which freight working has been speeded up in North America, as well as in France, Germany, and other European countries, has been by fitting all the freight wagons with 'continuous' brakes — actually, compressed air brakes are used in these countries — so making it possible for the driver to apply the brakes throughout the whole length of a freight train even a mile or more long. For this reason, American freight trains, despite their enormous length, can be, and frequently are, worked at speeds of a mile-a-minute and more, perfectly under control. In Great Britain, however, on many of the slower freight trains, such as those carrying coal, the only brakes that can be applied while the train is in motion are those on the engine and tender, and on the guard's van at the rear. For this reason the speeds of such trains

The most powerful steam locomotives in the world are the immense articulated 'Big Boy' class of the Union Pacific R.R., 4-8-8-4 locomotives which with their 14-wheel tenders weigh 540 tons apiece in full running order. No. 4019 is climbing to a summit level of 8,013 ft. at Sherman, west of Cheyenne, Wyoming. It is common on the easier American main lines to make up freight trains of well over 100 bogie wagons, a mile or more in length.

143

As with passenger trains, diesel-electric locomotives are taking over most of the long-distance freight working in the United States. This train of the Denver & Rio Grande Western R.R., winding away out of sight on the far right of the picture, is running through Ruby Canyon of the Colorado River. The principal main line of this railway climbs to 10,239 ft. altitude in the Tennessee Pass, and to 9,239 ft. on the Moffat Tunnel cut-off.

must be kept at a very much lower level, for stopping them is a so much more lengthy business.

A certain number of fast freight trains are run in this country, more especially at night, and some of these have the continuous brake from end to end, as you can see for yourselves by noting whether or not there are the vacuum hose-pipes connecting each van with the next. These trains are composed generally of covered or 'box' wagons, and, like their American counterparts, can run at anything up to 60 miles per hour, where conditions are favourable. A number of other British freight trains are allowed to travel at higher speeds than the slow mineral trains by having half-a-dozen or more wagons with continuous brakes coupled up next to the engine and tender, which increases the braking power on the train and gives the driver better control of his load.

The guard's van of a freight train is a capacious vehicle, as the guard has to ride in it sometimes for hours at a stretch. To keep him warm in winter weather, a coal-fired stove is provided, and this explains the smoke that may be seen drifting from the van chimney. In America the caboose, or 'crummy', as it is known in railwaymen's slang, is far bigger; it may have to accommodate four or five men, and so has a cooking stove, bunks for comfortable night travel, a desk for the conductor to do his work, and, in the latest cabooses, a diesel-electric set to provide power for the lighting and for the radio sets I have described already.

The caboose is carried on eight wheels, and usually has a raised section in the middle, with glass windows all round, called a 'cupola'; inside the cupola there are raised seats in which members of the crew can sit, and so see over the top of the highest wagons in the train. Where the railway is very curved, as in mountain country, long periods may pass without the train crew in the caboose catching sight of the engine, because of the length of the trains, but in these

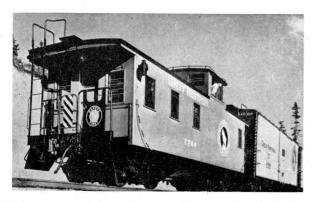

The American guard's van for freight trains, known as a caboose or 'crummy', is much larger than its British counterpart, and is always carried on eight wheels. The raised 'cupola' is to give the crew a clear view over the top of the train.

A standard British brake van for freight trains. It is provided with a coal-fired stove and facilities for cooking in its comfortable interior. The weight of the van is increased by iron weights to 20 tons, for assistance in braking.

days the radio enables them to keep in touch with one another in a way that was never possible before.

There are many different kinds of freight trains. The fastest freights run to timetable, just like the passenger trains, and punctual working is very important, because they carry all

The crew of an American caboose may have to travel in it for extended periods, and so much is done to make it comfortable for them. This Chicago & North Western 'way car' contains bunks, a desk (far right-hand corner) for writing work, a large stove with cooking facilities and a table for meals, and double windows to keep out the cold. The conductor looks justifiably proud of the spotless cleanliness of his travelling home.

kinds of commodities, usually overnight, that need to be in the shops in good time on the following morning. The rest of the freight service, for the most part, is moved under the instructions of 'Control'.

At the principal junctions on most main lines there are the control offices, connected by telephone with every station and signalbox over the length of main line for which the control office concerned is responsible. On the wall of each control office there is a kind of map of the stretch of line controlled, showing each running line, and every siding and loop. The trains are represented by pins which can be plugged into the map, to show where each freight train that is running or standing in the area under control may be found at any given moment. Attached to these pins are tabs which carry the number of the engine, the number of wagons, the names of the crew, the time they began duty, and other details concerning the train concerned. So the trains are handled by this central 'brain' somewhat in the same way that pieces are moved on a chessboard, and all the necessary information is received from and communicated to the signal boxes by telephone.

At a given time each morning, there is a conference by telephone of all the control officers along the main line, so that a general picture of how the traffic is working may be exchanged. There are times when large goods yards are receiving too much traffic, and tend to get blocked; if that is the case, there is no use continuing to run traffic towards those yards, or the main lines would get choked with trains waiting their turn to be received. So trains may be parked in sidings well down the main line, under instructions from the controllers, until the normal flow of traffic can be resumed: this kind of thing is arranged at the controllers' conferences. The control system has revolutionized freight working.

How does an individual wagon make its way from, say, the small station of Puddleton to a station on the other side of the country called, we will imagine, Much Binding? Once a day there pursues its leisurely way along the branch on which Puddleton is found, what is called a 'pick-up goods'; its business is what its name suggests, to pick up all the odd wagons that are waiting in readiness at the various stations along the line, and, just as the postman collects letters from the various pillarboxes to carry them to a central sorting office, to work the wagons to a central marshalling yard where they can be sorted out according to their many different destinations. So the pick-up goods stops at Puddleton; the engine is uncoupled and dives into the goods yard, attaching our wagon for Much Binding and any others that may be ready; it pulls them out and couples them on to the train, which then continues on its way.

The destination of the pick-up goods, as I have said, is a marshalling yard where the wagons are all to be sorted out. In earlier days this was done, and in the smaller yards it still is done, by shunting engines which, in their jerky fashion, push the pick-up goods train towards the sidings, and then stop suddenly, while individual wagons, which have been uncoupled by shunters, pass into one siding or another — the shunters moving the necessary switches — according to their destinations. Over and over again the string of wagons has to be pulled out before the backing can take place, and all this takes a long time.

The bigger marshalling yards have much more modern methods. Long ago someone thought

A modern marshalling yard, looking down from the crest of the hump. On the left a cut of two wagons is passing through one of the rail-brakes, or retarders, which check the speed of the wagons as they enter the sidings, to prevent violent impacts. Six retarders in all can be seen. The yard shown is one laid out recently by the Union Pacific R.R. at Pocatello, Idaho, on its main line to Portland, Oregon.

out how the force of gravity might come to the aid of shunting, and this was the beginning of what are known as 'hump' marshalling yards. The track along which the pick-up goods is pushed towards the sidings is made to rise gradually toward a crest, and on the far side of this summit the line drops very steeply towards the switches that give access towards the various sidings.

As the train is pushed over the hump, the wagons are uncoupled one by one, and the moment they are over the summit they draw quickly away from one another down the steep slope on the other side. So it is possible for shunters to move the switches smartly between wagon and wagon, directing them to their proper sidings, and all the fussy business of drawing the train out and pushing it back, over and over again, is done away with.

Still more modern are the great marshalling yards that are completely mechanized, as, for example, those of the Eastern Region at March, in Cambridgeshire, or the London Midland Region at Toton, near Nottingham, or the North Eastern Region at Hull. Here electricity has been brought in to speed up the working in all kinds of ingenious ways.

Let us suppose that the pick-up goods with our wagon from Puddleton to Much Binding has arrived at the vast Toton yard, and let us see what happens to it there. First of all, a shunter walks along the length of the train, examining the label on each wagon which shows

In a present-day marshalling yard, and especially the busier ones, the work of sorting wagons must go on day and night in order to keep pace with the flow of the traffic. Brilliant lighting is therefore essential for the night work, and a fine example is seen here in Toton yard of the London Midland Region, just north of Trent Junction on the Midland main line to the north. The view is taken from the crest of one of the humps.

where it is going, and then chalking a big number on the wagon end. It is the number of the particular siding into which that wagon is to be shunted.

Now the 'humping engine' — probably a powerful diesel which can be run steadily at a very low speed — begins to push the pick-up goods so that presently the end wagon reaches the crest of the hump. In the 'hump room' the operator looks for the chalked number on the end, and presses a correspondingly numbered button on the operating table in front of him. This button electrically works, first the 'King' points, where the line divides into two; then the 'Queen' points, where the two branch into four; and, last, the 'Jack' points, where the four multiply themselves into thirty-two sidings all told.

So the road is set automatically for the wagon, which is now running quite fast, for the gradient off the top of the hump at first is as steep as 1 in 18, and then gradually flattens out. One by one the wagons are following one another, each drawing quickly away from the next as it starts to run downhill, and giving time for the movement of the switches between wagon and wagon. Thus, without being touched by hand, our wagon makes its way into the siding which holds wagons for the Much Binding branch.

Now a certain precaution has to be taken as the wagons run into their sidings. The sidings gradually fill up, until the time comes to clear each one; and if a loaded wagon were to run fast off the hump into a siding nearly full of wagons, there might be such a 'biff' that not only the wagon loads, but the wagons themselves, might be seriously damaged. Some means must be provided for slowing the wagons down; and it would be very wasteful if an army of shunters were needed to run beside the moving wagons and pin the brakes down one by one. A way has now been devised, known as the 'rail-brake', of braking each wagon

At Toton yard, a diesel-electric shunter pushes a freight train, already uncoupled into its various 'cuts', over the top of the hump.

The steep incline from the hump down which the 'cuts' of wagons accelerate fast enough to enable the switches to be moved between them.

One of the rail-brakes, or retarders, which grip the wagon wheels and slow them down before the 'cut' enters one of the reception sidings.

separately, as it passes by, from the control tower.

Between the 'Queen' points and the 'Jack' points we find these rail-brakes, which form part of the track. Just over 70 feet in length, they grip the wagon wheels on both sides as the wagons run through. If the grip is a tight one, the wagon is slowed considerably; if less pressure is applied, it will continue to run for a long distance. The man in the control tower who is in charge of the braking has to keep a careful eye on each siding, in order to see how far each wagon has to run before it comes up to the wagons that are in that siding already; and he applies the rail-brakes accordingly. In these mechanized ways the work of sorting at big yards has been speeded up tremendously; at Toton, in the down yard alone, it is nothing to handle five thousand wagons in a single day.

After these adventurous proceedings, we find our Much Binding wagon in the siding which is collecting all the wagons for the Much Binding branch, and, probably, various other destinations in the same area.

From Toton it will doubtless form part of a 'through' freight train which will run to another marshalling yard in the Much Binding direction without putting wagons on or off during the journey: then will come more sorting; and finally another 'pick-up goods' will take charge of it, and work it along the branch until at last it is deposited in the Much Binding goods yard, its long journey at an end.

CHAPTER 13

Signals and signalling

IT would not be possible, in the space of one brief chapter, to go into all the complexities of present-day railway signalling, and we must content ourselves with looking at some of its most important features. The purpose of signalling is to keep the trains moving in safety — and, above all, to keep them *moving*. When trains first began to run, their speeds were so low that it was sufficient for safe running to see that so many minutes elapsed before one train was allowed to follow another; but as speeds increased, it soon became necessary to change the time interval to a space interval. This was the origin of the 'block system' of signalling.

The principle of block working is that there shall never be less than the length of what is called a 'block section' between any two trains running on the same track. Entry into a section is governed by the signalbox which separates it from the previous section, through the medium of what are curiously misnamed 'fixed signals', to distinguish them from the signals which

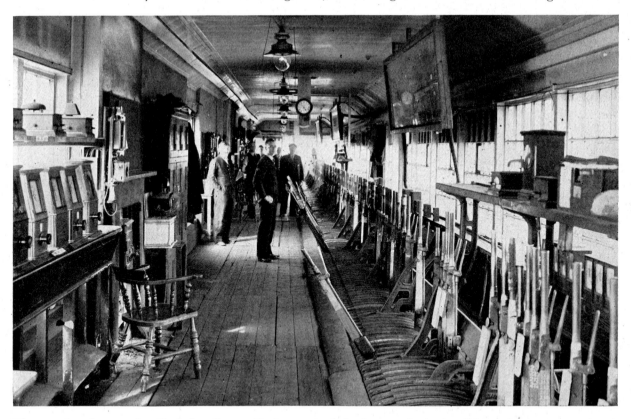

The one-time Locomotive Yard signalbox at York contained the longest single signal frame in the country, with 240 levers in one continuous row. This was but one of a number of boxes at York which were superseded when the new all-electric installation shown opposite was brought into use in 1952. The elimination of physical labour needs no stress. On the left are the old bell-signalling block instruments.

The modern electric 'signalbox' at York controlling all signalling and switch movements throughout from Chaloner's Whin Junction, 2 miles to the south, to Skelton, 1½ miles to the north. At the top of the four-sided diagram are the describers announcing the approach of trains; the diagram itself shows all the lines controlled, with every signal and switch. As soon as a route has been 'set', it is illuminated from end to end on the diagram by white lights; each train, as it moves through the area, shows exactly where it is by the lighting up of red lights. Below the diagram are the hundreds of operating switches and buttons; the four signalmen never actually see the trains whose movements they control. In the view below are the maze of tracks at the south approach to York station, the main lines to the right and the goods lines to the left.

Derby Control Office — one of many that control the working of British Railways freight traffic. Each train standing or moving in the area controlled has its small record card, inscribed with the number of the engine, the number of wagons, the names of driver, fireman and guard, and other details; this is plugged into its approximate position on the long track diagram above the operators, who are in telephone communication with every signalbox and yard in the area.

previously were given to drivers by hand. Actually the so-called fixed signals are either movable semaphore arms on posts, with spectacles moving in front of lamps to give corresponding light indications at night, or, in the most modern signalling, electric 'colour-lights' only. Colour-light signals can be seen from a considerably greater distance away than the semaphore arms, even in broad daylight, and it is only considerations of cost that prevent the former from being used on a far wider scale than at present.

Into almost every detail of signalling there enters that versatile servant of man — electricity. From the earliest days of railway signalling, means had to be found for the signalmen in adjacent boxes to communicate with one another, and electricity solved the problem. A code of bell signalling was devised, using single-stroke bells, and if you stand anywhere near a box you cannot fail to hear the 'conversation' that takes place on these bells at the approach of any train. There is first the enquiry 'Is line clear' (four beats on the bell in even succession if it is an express passenger or 'Class A' train; three beats–pause–one beat for a slow passenger or 'Class B' train) from the box next in rear, and then, in a few minutes time, the 'train entering section' (two beats), which means that the train is now actually passing the previous box.

While the signalman is acknowledging each bell signal by repeating it back on his bell circuit

TYPES OF SIGNALS

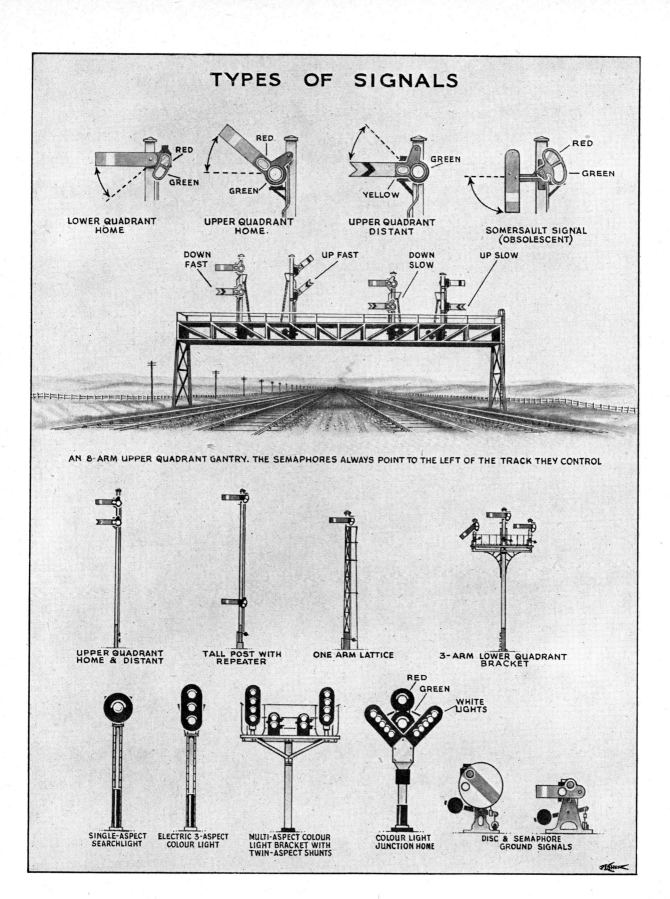

LOWER QUADRANT HOME.

UPPER QUADRANT HOME.

UPPER QUADRANT DISTANT

SOMERSAULT SIGNAL (OBSOLESCENT)

RED
GREEN

RED
GREEN

GREEN
YELLOW

RED
GREEN

DOWN FAST

UP FAST

DOWN SLOW

UP SLOW

AN 8-ARM UPPER QUADRANT GANTRY. THE SEMAPHORES ALWAYS POINT TO THE LEFT OF THE TRACK THEY CONTROL

UPPER QUADRANT HOME & DISTANT

TALL POST WITH REPEATER

ONE ARM LATTICE

3-ARM LOWER QUADRANT BRACKET

RED
GREEN
WHITE LIGHTS

SINGLE-ASPECT SEARCHLIGHT

ELECTRIC 3-ASPECT COLOUR LIGHT

MULTI-ASPECT COLOUR LIGHT BRACKET WITH TWIN-ASPECT SHUNTS

COLOUR LIGHT JUNCTION HOME

DISC & SEMAPHORE GROUND SIGNALS

to the box which has sent it, at the same time he is manipulating his block instrument in such a way that the needle on the dial shows him, first, that he has 'accepted' the train, and then, after receiving the 'train entering section' rings, that it is actually 'on line' between the next box and his own. Meantime he has been conducting the same bell conversation with the signalman in the box next beyond him, and on obtaining 'line clear', he has lowered his signals, so permitting the driver of the train to enter the block section which this particular box controls. The sequence of bell ringing is concluded by the signalman sending 'train out of section' (two beats–pause–one beat) to the signalman in rear of him as the train passes his box, and restoring the needle of his block instrument to 'line blocked', which is its normal position.

The signals themselves, of which the principal types in use are illustrated on page 153, now need attention. It is easy to distinguish between the two main classes of semaphore signal — the 'stop' and the 'distant' — because the side of the former that faces the driver is painted red, whereas the latter is painted yellow. Also the outer end of the stop signal arm is square, but that of the distant arm is cut into the shape of a fishtail. At night, the glass spectacle which moves in front of a lighted lamp, in conjunction with the movement of the arm, shows green in both cases when the arm is pulled off, but red for the stop signal when in the horizontal position, and yellow for the distant signal.

As with the colour-lights at road intersections, yellow is a 'caution' indication. So, as you have no doubt noticed, if a driver approaches a distant signal at 'caution' — that is, with the yellow arm horizontal, or showing the yellow light at night — he does not stop his train. But you will see that he has shut off steam and is preparing to stop if necessary. For the distant signal, which stands from $\frac{1}{2}$-mile to $\frac{3}{4}$-mile away from the box that controls it, gives the driver an advance indication of the position of the stop signals immediately adjacent to the box. If the distant signal is pulled off, then all the stop signals at the box also are off, and the driver may continue at full speed. But if the distant signal is at 'caution', then the driver is warned that the next stop signals are at danger, and is given ample time and space in which to pull up his train.

Under the floor of the signalbox there is a complicated piece of mechanism called the locking table, which is designed to prevent the signalman from making errors that might result in accidents. By a system of steel slides, notches and tappets, levers can be locked in position, and by this means the signalman cannot pull over the lever working a distant signal until the levers controlling the stop signals for the same track also have been pulled over. The locking also is used to prevent the movement of switches and signals which might permit trains to cross one another's tracks, especially at junctions.

One class of line on which collisions might very easily occur but for the special precautions taken is the single line, used by trains running in both directions. The driver of any train running over a single line in Great Britain has to be in possession of a token. The original type of token was a single tablet, and collision was made impossible because no two drivers could hold the same tablet at the same time. But the frequent necessity to run a second or

By means of 'centralized traffic control' or 'C.T.C.', the working of freight trains over single lines of great length can now be controlled from one central office, from which the switches admitting to the loops at which trains pass one another, and all the signals, are worked electrically. In this view three control machines are seen in one Santa Fe office at Amarillo, Texas, which signals 310 miles of line from Waynoka to Clovis. Each operator has before him an illuminated diagram of the section of line that he controls, with the switches under for working signals and points. Freight train working has been greatly speeded up in this way.

third train in the one direction before a train ran in the other direction, so enabling the token to be returned to the starting point, resulted in the evolution of electrical token systems which have solved this difficulty.

Electric block instruments at both ends of the single track store between them a number of tokens, but by electrical control it is impossible to withdraw a token from either instrument until another token has been fed into either one instrument or the other. On single-track main lines, such as that of the Highland line, the engines are fitted with special apparatus which catches and delivers the tokens at station and other passing loops without the reduction of speed that was necessary in earlier days, when all tokens had to be exchanged by hand.

There is another way in which electricity is made to enter into the task of protecting trains. In many signalboxes on the quieter stretches of line, there is no automatic protection against a signalman pulling off his signals for a second train when the preceding train is still running, or perhaps has been brought to a stand by a breakdown or some other cause, in his section. At times, by some unaccountable lapse, a signalman has forgotten the presence of a train or engine actually standing at his box, and by lowering his signals has allowed a second train to come into collision. But at all the busier boxes such casualties are now made impossible by what is called 'track-circuit'.

Modern signalbox design is a great advance on that of earlier days. This all-electric French box replaces five previous manually-operated boxes, over 6 miles of line, and can signal a total of 350 different routes.

A long stretch of line adjacent to the box is electrified by passing a weak current through the rails of the track, which are carefully insulated from one another, and from all adjacent tracks. If any train is running or standing on the electrified section, a short circuit is completed from one rail to the other through the wheels and axles, and breaks down a relay.

This is used to impose a lock on the lever or levers which would permit the signalman to admit a

The illuminated track diagram and the operating table of the Montereau all-electric signalling installation. The appropriate track on the diagram lights up when any train is moving or standing on it. Again the saving of labour, as compared with the old manual working, must be emphasized; moreover, the moving of one or two thumb-switches may be enough to set a road that needed half-a-dozen or more heavy lever movements before.

second train to the occupied line, to work visual 'line occupied' indicators, and for other purposes.

The busiest lines of all are track-circuited continuously, and over them the track-circuits actually work the signals; that is to say, except at junctions the human element is dispensed with and the trains signal themselves. Apart from such automatic signalling, which was described in Chapter 7 in connection with railways underground, it would be impossible to work trains at intervals of no more than 90 seconds, which is the frequency on several London tube lines at the rush hours. To a limited extent, automatic signalling is used also on British main lines, as, for example, on the principal main line of the North Eastern Region between York and Darlington, but in this respect Great Britain is far behind the United States, which has thousands of miles of line automatically signalled, both with semaphore signals and colour-lights.

Great progress has been made in the U.S.A., also, in the direct control of trains from the signals. On a number of main lines, by means of what is described as 'continuous inductive' electric signalling, the locomotive driver has in front of him in the cab a panel which continuously shows green, for a clear road, but changes to yellow or double yellow for caution, and to red for stop. Not only so, but in the event of yellow or red, the brakes are applied automatically to slow down or stop the train. Apart from tube and other electric lines fitted with automatic train-stopping apparatus, as described in Chapter 7, the only British applications of automatic train control have been those of the late Great Western Railway, now the Western Region, the London, Midland & Scottish installation (now Eastern Region) between Fenchurch Street and Southend-on-Sea, and the experimental installation by British Railways between King's Cross and Huntingdon.

The two latter are a close approximation to the American inductive signalling method, but the Western Region method is simpler. It consists of a ramp, seen between the rails of the track, working in conjunction with the distant signal. If the distant signal is pulled off to 'clear', the ramp is electrified, and the contacting shoe under the locomotive picks up the current, ringing a bell in the engine cab. If the signal is at caution, however, and the ramp is 'dead', a loud horn sounds in the cab, and a partial brake application is made automatically.

The value to a driver of audible signalling of this kind, in foggy weather especially, needs no emphasis. Once again it is the bugbear of cost that prevents the wider adoption of such advanced signalling methods as these.

The same applies, as already mentioned, to the substitution of colour-light for semaphore signalling, though considerable advances have been made in this direction. You may have noticed that many of the colour-light installations have signals showing not only red, green and yellow indications, but a 'double yellow' as well. The corresponding indications to the driver are red for stop, single yellow for one section ahead clear only, double yellow for two sections ahead clear, and green to continue at full speed. While the double yellow calls for caution, it enables dense traffic to continue in motion at a higher speed than the more cautious running compelled by single yellow indications would permit.

Often colour-light signals may be seen at isolated points along our main lines. In some cases

Originally all semaphore signals were worked by wires from manually-operated lever frames, and vast numbers of such signals remain in operation. But electricity now has come into use extensively, making it possible to work signals from far greater distances from a box than previously. The Canadian Pacific signals in this photograph, being passed by a transcontinental express near Field, British Columbia, are operated by electric motors attached to the top of the tubular posts, behind the arms. The semaphores are of the upper quadrant type, rising to the vertical position for 'clear'.

they have made it possible to dispense with intermediate signal boxes, and in many places they have been substituted for semaphore distant signals, for these days of increasing speeds make it necessary to give drivers warning at greater distances from signal boxes than ever previously. Some colour-light signals are worked by ordinary lever-frames in signal boxes, as, for example, those down the Western Region main line out of Paddington. But more commonly the working is entirely electric, and some of the modern electric signalling installations at big terminal stations, junctions and traffic centres are amazing in their ingenuity and complexity. Among the chief of these may be mentioned Waterloo, London Bridge, Victoria, Cannon Street, Liverpool Street, King's Cross, and Paddington stations in London; Bristol (Temple Meads), Crewe, Doncaster, Edinburgh (Waverley), Glasgow (St. Enoch), and, most outstanding of all, the new installation at York.

In almost every case, the all-electric signalboxes combine the working of what were a number of independent boxes previously. In the earlier of them, the traditional lever-frames of full-length levers have been replaced by rows of miniature levers which can be pulled over by a flick of the finger and thumb. The precise condition of the track controlled by each box can be seen in a great diagram of the lines, which stands above the lever frame, and on which the position of every moving or standing train, engine, or vehicle is seen by means of tiny lamps which light up. Incorporated in the signalling system, as with an ordinary mechanically-operated box, is an elaborate system of locking, only in this case all-electric.

In the latest installations, however, the operation of points and signals is carried out on the diagram itself, by means of thumb-switches. The movement of a couple of these switches, located on the diagram adjacent to the track to which they refer, will 'set a road', with all the appropriate switches and signals, right through a station from one end to the other — provided all the lines concerned are clear, of course — doing in a matter of seconds what previously might have required a dozen or more hefty movements of full-size levers. What this means in economy of time and physical effort needs no stress. These great all-electric boxes have made it possible to reduce considerably the number of signalmen needed to work the traffic, though this reduction in part is balanced by the increase in the number of electric linemen required to keep in order the extremely complicated electric equipment, with its thousands of relays and other details.

The new signal box at York — or control room, as it is better described — with all its equipment has cost £500,000. It combines in one frame what previously was done by eight signalboxes with 867 mechanical levers; and a staff of 27 does in far less time what 70 men did previously. All the lines entering York, from four miles south to one mile north of the station, are controlled from this one central point, which is able to set up the staggering total of 827 different routes! At Chaloner's Whin Junction, where the main line for London diverges from the Leeds line, there was previously a large signalbox containing 44 levers; today all the work of this junction is done by twelve route switches on the signalling panel, controlling no more than five signals.

In the relay room there are over 400 *miles* of wire, serving more than 1,000 locking relays and more than 2,000 other relays; the majority of the lock relays have up to 108 terminals apiece. In the ordinary course, the great signalling panel is worked by four men, under the direction of a traffic regulator who sits at a desk facing the panel. Such is the service rendered by electricity to modern signalling.

With the increasing speed of trains, the urgent need is realized of simplifying the signalling to the maximum degree possible, at junctions especially, in order that the driver of a fast-moving train shall have a minimum of difficulty in picking out the particular signal or signals that refer to his train. Older readers may remember the immense gantries of semaphore signals that once spanned all tracks at Rugby, at the east end of Newcastle Central station, outside Waterloo, and at many other busy stations. Today a single colour-light signal, with an illuminated number showing which particular track is set, may replace a dozen or more individual semaphore arms previously used at the same location. At junctions, too, the place of the separate semaphores that once indicated whether a train was to proceed directly ahead or to diverge to the left or the right, has been taken by rows of white lights above a colour-light signal, which light up, pointing diagonally to left or right, if the train is to branch to the

left or right respectively.

To traffic control offices I have referred already, in Chapter 12. They help to make the best possible use of engines and men, to prevent congestion at key points, and above all, to keep the traffic moving.

These two views illustrate the automatic control of trains on the tube and other lines of London Transport. When the signal is in the clear position, the lineside trip lever, working electrically in conjunction with the adjacent signal, lies out of action, pulling against the horizontal spring shown in the lower view. When the signal is at danger, the trip is released, and is pulled by the spring to the vertical position, where it can intercept the lever below the motorcoach of the train, as shown above; this interception cuts off the current and applies the brakes, in the event of a driver trying to pass the signal at danger.

CHAPTER 14

To the clouds by train

IT is amazing to think of high-speed streamline trains making their way over mountain summits nearly twice as lofty as the highest mountains in Britain; yet this is a commonplace in the United States. A little to the west of Cheyenne, Wyoming, the busy main line of the Union Pacific Railroad, over which there pass three famous streamliners daily on their way from Chicago to Los Angeles, San Francisco and Portland, and many other expresses too, climbs to 8,013 feet above the sea at Sherman. Further to the south there is the main line of the Atchison, Topeka & Santa Fe, also with its streamliners, which has four summit levels of over 7,000 feet, the highest of them in the Raton tunnel, 7,573 feet up.

All the American main lines that run through to the Pacific coast have to make their way through the Rocky Mountains and other mountain ranges, in some cases for a thousand miles continuously. The main line record is held by the Denver & Rio Grande Western, which connects the capitals of Colorado and Utah, Denver and Salt Lake City, by 570 miles of main line which at no point is lower than the 4,000 foot contour, and at its highest reaches 9,239 feet in the Moffat Tunnel. Before this 6¼-mile tunnel was bored, the trains had to pass over an even loftier altitude in the Tennessee Pass, 10,239 feet above the sea.

But even these heights pale beside those of some of the South American railways which have been driven up into the heart of the Andes in search of the mineral wealth of Chile, Peru and Bolivia. This is where all the world's record railway altitudes are found. The great mountain chain of the Andes runs the whole length of the Pacific coast of South America, and the principal railways start from the ports, such as Callao, Mollendo and Antofagasta, and then drive straight up into the mountains to astonishing heights.

The Peruvian Central is the most outstanding of these lines. It begins on the Pacific at Callao, the port of Lima, capital of Peru. Climbing steadily, in the first 54 miles from Callao to Chosica the train has lifted itself nearly 3,000 feet above sea level; but this is nothing to what happens in the next 118 miles. For as the train makes its way laboriously through Galera tunnel, 172 miles by rail from the coast, it has reached the immense height of 15,694 feet above the sea.

Much of the ascent is on gradients as steep as 1 in 30 and even 1 in 25; the precipitous mountain sides are ascended by zigzagging to and fro, with reversals of the trains at each elbow bend. Cylinders of oxygen have to be carried in the trains for the relief of any travellers who may suffer from mountain sickness because of the tremendous changes of altitude through which they pass in so short a time. The line proceeds to Huancayo, 346 miles from Callao, through a region some 10,000 to 11,000 feet up, which is the finest wheat-growing district in Peru.

From its lofty location near Hohtenn, 1,300 ft. above the Rhone valley, the Lötschberg main line begins its 12-mile descent to join at Brigue the Simplon main line, far below to the left. Many viaducts and tunnels were needed on this spectacular stretch of line.

At Ticlio, not far from the summit, a loop line branches off which gets to the even higher level of 15,806 feet at La Cima. This is nearly, but not quite, the world's record for altitude, which is held by the Antofagasta (Chile) & Bolivia Railway; the Collahuassi branch of the latter touches 15,817 feet — practically level with the top of Mont Blanc — at Montt. The main line of this railway, on its way to La Paz, is never below the 12,000-feet level for 500 miles on end! And who would like to be the stationmaster at Condor, on the Potosi branch, highest railway station in the world at 15,705 feet? It must be remembered, however, that here in the Andes we are no great distance from the Equator, so that in a normal summer the lines can be completely free from snow and ice even when above the 15,000-feet contour.

A railway steamer which sailed across the Atlantic and made its way up into the Andes, to take up a regular service on a lake 120 miles long and 12,500 feet above the sea, is another curiosity in this area. It is the *S.S. Inca*, belonging to the Peruvian Southern Railway; the vessel was built at Hull, worked under her own steam across the Atlantic, round Cape Horn, and up the Pacific to the Peruvian port of Mollendo, where she was dismantled and carried in pieces up the Peruvian Southern to the port of Puno, on Lake Titicaca, the most amazing sheet of water of its size anywhere in the world. Here the *Inca* was reassembled and launched on the lake in 1905. In all, twenty-four railway summits exceeding 12,000 feet in altitude may be found in the Andes.

All the railways of which we have been thinking in South America are worked by ordinary adhesion methods — that is, by the grip of the locomotive driving wheels on the running rails. The steepest gradient yet mentioned has been 1 in 25, but in various parts of the world mountain railways are worked by adhesion on much steeper inclinations than this. In Switzerland, for example, there is the Montreux-Oberland Bernois Railway, which loops to and fro on the steep mountainside above Montreux, on the Lake of Geneva, with a gradient which for miles is as steep as 1 in 14. The Bernina Railway, which lifts itself 6,000 feet in the 25 miles from Tirano to the Bernina Hospice, also has a long stretch of 1 in 14 from Poschiavo up to the station at Alp Grüm, immediately opposite the great Palü glacier. This line, by the way, attains to 7,403 feet altitude near the Bernina Pass, and is the highest through railway route in Europe.

But some of the climbs over passes or to mountain summits would have been prohibitively

The famous Landwasser Viaduct, on the Rhaetian Railway main line from Chur to St. Moritz, Switzerland. The last right-hand arch takes its springing direct from the precipice wall, and trains emerging from the tunnel find themselves immediately on the full 230 ft. height of the viaduct.

Coming eastwards from San Francisco, the 'Overland' main line of the Southern Pacific R.R. has a tremendous ascent to reach the Continental Divide. At Sacramento it is 35 ft. above sea level; at Norden, 102 miles east, it is 7,018 ft. up. Here the 'City of San Francisco' streamliner is climbing through Emigrant Gap on its 2,257-mile journey from Oakland Pier, San Francisco, to Chicago, headed with a 6,000 h.p. triple-unit diesel-electric locomotive.

costly unless much steeper gradients than this had been used. As steepness increases, we have two risks to bear in mind — first, that the locomotives will no longer have sufficient grip on the rails to make climbing possible, and, second, that the trains will slide down the hills out of control when making the descent. Both assistance to the locomotives and protection for the trains are therefore necessary. Rack-and-pinion working solves the problem.

The rack, which is securely anchored down in the centre of the track, between the running rails, takes various forms, most of which originated in Switzerland. The older, or Riggenbach, type is like a steel ladder laid flat; the later Abt rack is a double row of steel teeth set up on edge and out of step with one another; and, on the very steepest lines, there is the Locher system, in which the rack has two rows of teeth projecting horizontally from a centre rail. Under the locomotives there are toothed pinion driving wheels, so that the movement of the locomotive is not by means of adhesion on the ordinary running rails, but by the driving pinions engaging with the rack. Under each coach of a rack railway, also, there is a pinion which engages with the rack, and so protects the coach from any attempt to get out of control even on the steepest inclines.

On many through railways in the Alps and elsewhere, rack-and-pinion working is needed only on the steepest inclines, such as those over the mountain passes. On lines of this description the locomotives use their ordinary driving wheels over the flatter parts of the line, and run their trains at speeds of 30 to 40 miles per hour. Then, as a rack section is approached, the train is slowed down to a walking pace as all the pinions are engaged, and proceeds at a very limited speed up or down the rack. In recent years, however, with their powerful modern electric locomotives, some of the Swiss railways have greatly speeded up their rack-and-pinion working.

On the Brünig Railway, between Lucerne and Interlaken, for example, or the Furka-Oberalp, between Brigue, Andermatt and Disentis, trains of five to ten coaches — of very light rolling stock, of course — today are being hauled up inclines of 1 in

Highest point on the Atchison, Topeka & Santa Fe 2,226-mile main line from Chicago to Los Angeles is Raton Tunnel, 7,573 ft. above the sea, in the Rocky Mountains. At the post just to the right of the signal the train passes from Colorado into New Mexico.

11, 1 in 10, and even 1 in 9, at speeds up to 20 miles per hour. The exhilaration of climbing in a train at this speed needs to be felt to be believed. A record achieved by the Furka-Oberalp Railway, incidentally, is that of running a restaurant car in its trains, up and down 1 in 9! Two summer trains, one westbound, and the other eastbound, choose the bleak summit of the Oberalp Pass, 6,670 feet above the sea, to hand the precious vehicle over from one to the other!

Until now we have been thinking of railways which run trains of coaches with independent locomotives. There are also the purely mountain lines which operate with electric motor-coaches, possibly hauling or pushing one or two trailers, or running by themselves. With these, considerably steeper gradients are possible. In the Alps, 1 in 5 and 1 in 4 gradients are common on such lines.

The record for rack-and-pinion working is held by the railway which climbs from Alpnachstad, on the Lake of Lucerne, to the summit of Pilatus, whisking the passenger up through a difference in level of 5,344 feet — over a mile — in a journey just under $2\frac{3}{4}$ miles in length.

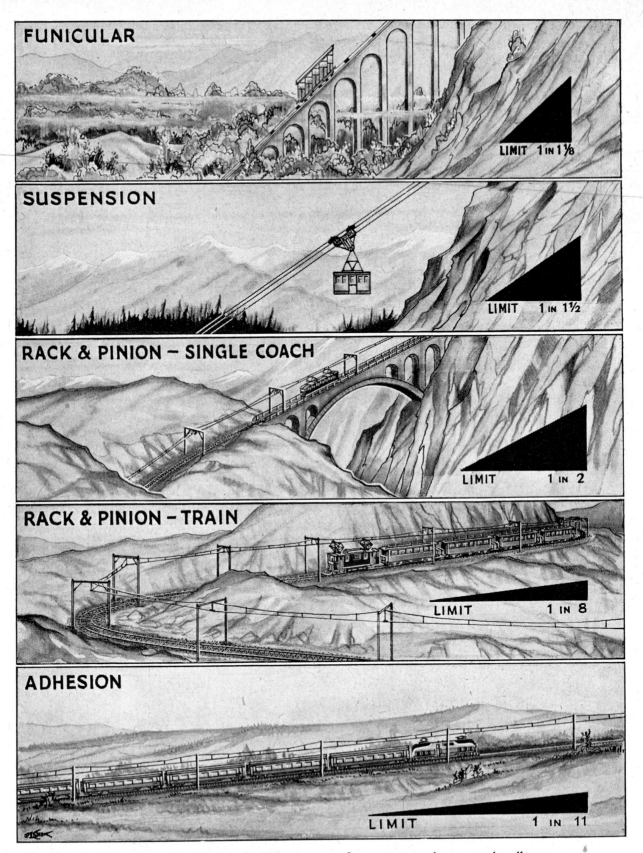

FUNICULAR

LIMIT 1 IN 1⅛

SUSPENSION

LIMIT 1 IN 1½

RACK & PINION – SINGLE COACH

LIMIT 1 IN 2

RACK & PINION – TRAIN

LIMIT 1 IN 8

ADHESION

LIMIT 1 IN 11

The steepest safe inclinations for different types of passenger-carrying mountain railways.

Another great climb is made by the 'Orange Express' of the South African Railways on its way from Cape Town up the higher interior plateau of South Africa, in parts at the 6,000 ft. level and over. The 15-coach train here is seen in Tulbagh Kloof, headed by one of the latest 4-8-2 locomotives.

The average gradient is thus about 1 in $2\frac{3}{4}$, and the steepest gradient is 1 in 2. This is a really breathless climb for the passenger, especially where the train crawls up the face of a sheer precipice below the Esel. The journey, which in steam days took 70 minutes, has been cut with the modern 50-seater electric motor-coaches to half-an-hour. On the Pilatus line the Locher type of rack is used, the motor-coaches being fitted with double horizontal driving pinions.

The highest railway in the Alps that is laid entirely in the open climbs from Zermatt, in the south of Switzerland, close to the Italian border, to the top of a rocky eminence known as the Gornergrat, where the upper terminus is 10,134 above sea level. For nearly five thousand feet upwards the two-car trains slowly make their way, largely up a 1 in 5 gradient, with views in every direction gradually widening until the passenger finds himself ringed round with snow and ice in every direction, as far as the eye can reach.

The Gornergrat is one of the most wonderful viewpoints in the world. Far below the rocky ridge of which the Gornergrat forms the extremity there is seen the great Gorner glacier;

When carrying a railway down a mountain valley, the engineer is often faced with an abrupt drop in the valley floor, and it is to keep pace with such changes of level, without unduly steepening the railway gradient, that the spiral tunnel is used. This view shows part of the celebrated spiral location of the Gotthard Railway, Switzerland, near Giornico. It was taken from the uppermost of the three levels of the line, showing the middle level, after passing through Piano Tondo spiral tunnel, turning leftwards into Travi spiral tunnel, and emerging from the latter at the bridge over the River Ticino.

soaring up on the opposite side are a line of the great ice-clad monarchs of the Valais Alps — Monte Rosa, the Lyskamm, the Breithorn, and then, a little further west, isolated and magnificent, the great granite pyramid of the Matterhorn. The trip to the Gornergrat is one of the most spectacular railway rides in Europe.

But it is not the highest. That distinction belongs to the Jungfrau Railway, in the Bernese Oberland, which carries its passengers into the heart of a world of ice and snow that they could not possibly reach otherwise unless they were competent Alpine climbers. Starting from the well-known town of Interlaken, three narrow-gauge railways in combination join in the task of lifting the traveller through a difference in level of some 9,500 feet, in a journey 20 miles in length, to deposit him finally on the Jungfraujoch — the saddle — covered with an enormously thick ice-cap, that separates the mountains known as the Jungfrau and the Mönch.

The main interest of the journey centres in the Jungfrau Railway proper, from the Scheidegg to the summit terminus; although it is barely six miles long, the difficulties of construction at this altitude were so enormous that sixteen years elapsed between the beginning and the

168

A rotary snowplough in action

On railways which pass over high altitudes, or are laid through country which is subject to severe winter conditions, drifting snow causes considerable difficulties in railway operation. Exposed stretches of line where drifting is almost inevitable or danger is to be feared from avalanches, often are roofed over permanently with shelters of timber or reinforced concrete; at other points, especially where the line is in a cutting, some protection may be given by massive 'snow fences' at the side of the line. But the high-lying lines also must provide themselves with means for clearing the tracks of snow. The ram type of plough, shouldering the snow to right and left as it is pushed forwards, can deal with drifts of 3 feet to 5 feet or so, but the deeper drifts call for a steam-driven rotary plough, of the type illustrated, here seen in use on the Canadian Pacific Railway main line in the Rockies.

Spiral railway development in the mountains

Where a railway is being carried through mountainous country, the upward inclination of a valley floor is often steeper than any gradient which could reasonably be surmounted by the locomotives working the line. A maximum steepness of gradient therefore is decided on, and the engineer must then have recourse to some remarkable expedients in order to preserve this gradient evenly, but still to provide for continuous running of the trains. A very striking example of engineering location work in Switzerland is seen in this drawing of the Rhaetian Railway main line making its way up the Albula Valley in order to reach St. Moritz, which is nearly 6,000 feet above the sea. Between Bergün and Preda the gradient is steepened to 1 in 29, but three completely spiral tunnels and four viaducts across the river have been needed to conquer a difference in altitude of 1,368 feet between two stations only $3\frac{3}{4}$ miles apart as the crow flies.

(FOR COLOUR PLATES OF ABOVE SEE OVER)

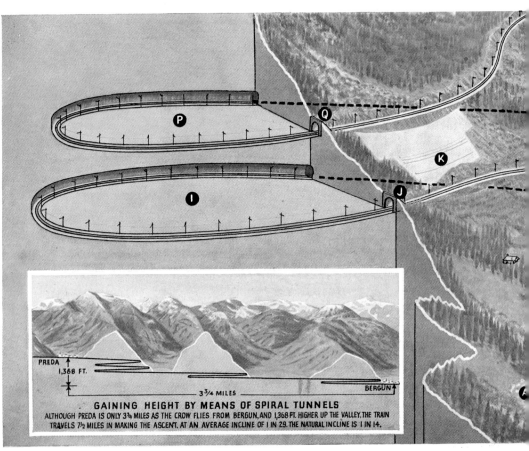

KEY TO LETTERING

Assuming we have left the loops on the open mountainside above Bergün station on our 1,368 feet climb to Preda, the key to the lettering is as follows: (A) The Albula River. (B) First viaduct over the river. (C) Entrance to first spiral tunnel. Motor road above. (D) Rugnux Tunnel — 724 yards long. (E) Tunnel exit. Line has climbed 80 feet in the spiral. (F) The 'Glacier Express', electrically operated. (G) Second viaduct crossing the Albula. (H) Entrance to second spiral tunnel. (I) Toua Tunnel — 740 yards long. (J) Tunnel exit, 75 feet higher up. (K) Concrete retaining wall. (L) Third viaduct crossing the Albula. (M) Spiral sweep on other side of valley. (N) Fourth viaduct crossing the Albula. (O) Entrance to third spiral tunnel. (P) Zuondra Tunnel — 586 yards long — immediately over the Toua Tunnel. (Q) Tunnel exit. (R) Line continues to climb to Preda.

GAINING HEIGHT BY MEANS OF SPIRAL TUNNELS

ALTHOUGH PREDA IS ONLY 3¾ MILES AS THE CROW FLIES FROM BERGÜN, AND 1,368 FT. HIGHER UP THE VALLEY, THE TRAIN TRAVELS 7½ MILES IN MAKING THE ASCENT, AT AN AVERAGE INCLINE OF 1 IN 29. THE NATURAL INCLINE IS 1 IN 14.

completion of the work. From the Scheidegg the train climbs straight towards the great rampart formed by the Eiger, the Mönch and the Jungfrau. At Eigergletscher station the train is hemmed in, on one side by the vast precipice, 6,000 feet high, that comes sweeping down from the summit of the Eiger, and on the other by the Eiger glacier. From here onwards, therefore, the engineers had to seek refuge in tunnel for $4\frac{1}{2}$ miles.

At first this tunnel is carried upwards just inside the face of the Eiger, and when the trains stop at Eigerwand, a station blasted out in the rock of the mountain, the passengers are led to windows, set at an almost incredible position high up the great precipice wall, from which they may look down on the village of Grindelwald, some 6,000 feet below them. At Jungfraujoch the railway finishes in a tunnel, at an altitude of 11,333 feet, the highest railway station in Europe. Here quite a colony has been established, with a large hotel, an observatory, and various other buildings, all linked by a labyrinth of tunnels that has been driven in the hard rock. So you can pass straight out on to the snow and ice covering the Jungfraujoch, without having had any of the strenuous exertion normally needed to climb far above the snow-line.

Climbing a 1 in 5 gradient on the Wengernalp Railway, Switzerland, with the aid of rack-and-pinion propulsion; the peaks in the background are the Eiger (left) and the Mönch, both over 13,000 ft. high. The Jungfrau Railway tunnels below these peaks, climbing from Kleine Scheidegg at 1 in 4 to reach Jungfraujoch, the mountain saddle at the extreme right of the picture, between the Mönch and the Jungfrau, where the terminus is 11,333 ft. above the sea. These new electric motorcoaches have cut the $6\frac{1}{2}$-mile journey from Lauterbrunnen up to the Kleine Scheidegg, with an ascent of 4,150 ft., from 70 to 40 minutes running time.

Steepest rack-and-pinion railway in the world is that up Pilatus, Switzerland, with a maximum inclination of 1 in 2; for safe operation this required the special Locher type of rack. The climb of 2¾ miles, from 1,434 ft. altitude at Alpnachstad to 6,778 ft. at Pilatuskulm, is completed in half-an-hour. This is a very popular excursion from Lucerne.

Until now the steepest gradient of any railway mentioned in this chapter has been 1 in 2, on the ascent of Pilatus, in Switzerland. This is about the limit of safety for rack and pinion working, but it is by no means the limit of steepness for Alpine mountain railways. With steeper gradients than 1 in 2, however, another method of traction must be used. It is familiar enough even to those of you who have never been outside England, for short railways of this kind may be seen up the cliffs at many of the resorts round our coasts. The cars are hauled upwards by wire ropes, and for economy in power, two cars are connected together by a single haulage cable that is passed round a winding drum at the head of the line, so that the descending car, assisted perhaps in weight by water ballast, may pull the ascending car up.

While few of the British 'funiculars' are much more than a hundred yards or so in length, some of the Alpine lines are over a mile long, which means more than a mile of moving cable, or twice that length and more if they are built with two or more independently-operated sections. A two-section line of this kind carries passengers up a mountain called the Niesen, in the Bernese Oberland region of Switzerland. The lower terminus at Mülenen is nearly 2¼ miles from the upper station, but there is a change of cars from one section to the other at an intermediate station called Schwandegg. In the course of the journey the passenger is lifted all but 5,400 feet, and when the line steepens near the summit to a gradient of 1 in 1½, the passenger in the car — if he has the courage to look out! — sees the valley of the Kander spread out below him exactly as if it were a map. The most horrifying stretch of all is the one near the summit on which the car crawls at 1 in 1½ over a viaduct — without any parapets!

So far as is known, the steepest funicular in public use is one in the Canton Ticino of Switzerland, which you can see when travelling south over the Gotthard main line, soon after leaving the lengthy Gotthard Tunnel. It was originally the works funicular used to carry materials to the storage lake level when the great Piotta power-station was under construction; later it was converted to a passenger line. As it climbs, it gradually steepens until the final section is at 88 per cent, or 1 in 1⅓.

However, I have beaten even that. Once, when another great hydro-electric power scheme was being carried out high up in the mountains of southern Switzerland, I was taken up the works funicular, which had a gradient of 108 per cent — steeper than 1 in 1, crawling like a fly up the wall in a wagon without any sides! It was a case of sitting tight and hoping for the best! !

A word is necessary, in concluding this chapter, about suspension lines. These are not really railways, as they have no rails; instead, their main supporting cables are swung from tower to tower, like mineral ropeways, and passenger cars, looking like a large size in bird-cages, and hanging from wheeled carriages which run on the cables, are hauled up the line from the bottom to the top. The 'funicular' principle is used, with the down-going car pulling the ascending car up. With an absence of permanent way, this is a cheap

Rope-worked or 'funicular' railways are limited in carrying capacity to two cars, and economize in power by the weight of the descending car being used to balance (by means of the continuous haulage cable) that of the ascending car. This is the Parsenn funicular, at Davos, Switzerland.

form of construction, for there are no tunnels or bridges to build; if a valley lies in the path of the *téléphérique*, as it is called, the ropeway is swung straight across it.

Probably the most unnerving of these lines is the one which French engineers have carried from Planpraz, a platform on the mountainside high above Chamonix, to the summit of the Brévent, a mountain immediately opposite to the towering mass of Mont Blanc. The face of the Brévent is a sheer cliff, so the engineers have calmly swung their cables straight across the yawning gap from Planpraz to the summit — a span of 4,400 feet with no intermediate support whatever. In the middle of this airy ascent, the passenger has nothing between himself and the nearest land, a thousand feet below, other than the quarter-inch or so of steel plate on which he is standing in the car!

Later developments of the *téléphérique* idea are the chair-lifts, up which passengers ride in single or double chairs. These are worked on the endless rope principle; either the chair hangers grip the rope, and the chairs run off on to runways at the top and bottom of the line

It is a breath-taking experience to travel up the funicular railway from Schattli to Stoos, in Central Switzerland, not far from the historic town of Schwyz. As this line approaches the summit terminus, seen in this view, the gradient steepens to 78 per cent (nearly 1 in 1¼), and the passenger finds himself looking down the sheer sides of a viaduct which the width of the passenger car actually overhangs!

so that passengers can get in and out in comfort, or there are the more primitive single-chair lines on which the chairs are attached to the rope permanently, so that their occupants must do acrobatic feats in getting into and out of the chairs while in motion. Swinging up in the sky in these frail chairs, with nothing but a slender bar latched across the front to hold the passenger in, is quite the most exciting of all forms of Alpine passenger transport!

A more recent development to be found on a suspension line which runs up to the 8,300 feet altitude of Bellalui, above Montana, carries its passengers completely enclosed in little four-seater cars, like sedan chairs, which are whisked out of and into the terminals by hooks suspended from an endless moving rope.

These *téléphériques* and chair-lifts have opened a new era in Alpine transport. Not only do they carry tourists and winter sports enthusiasts to high altitudes, but many remote and high-lying villages have been made easily accessible in this way. New lines of this kind are being opened every year, and are extremely popular.

On a suspension line, or *téléphérique*, passengers are swung from tower to tower in a travelling car. This Swiss line, from Gerschnialp to Trübsee (on the mountain edge immediately below the snow) has a final cable span of over 3,000 ft. without any intermediate support.

CHAPTER 15

The fight with nature—flood, frost and fog

In one way and another, the railways have a perpetual fight to wage against Nature. The particular ways by which Nature conducts her attacks are varied. In a country like Britain, the climate is such that fog will descend like a blanket, and make it almost, if not quite, impossible for drivers to see the signals, so that the working of the trains is badly slowed down. In regions which experience severe cold in the winter, snow, drifting on to the lines, especially in cuttings, can cause a complete hold-up of traffic until the tracks have been cleared. In mountainous areas the same snow, breaking loose high up in the mountains and falling down the mountainsides in vast masses at a speed greater than that of the fastest express trains, can not merely bury the trains but can cause serious disasters unless precautions are taken.

And then, in countries subject to torrential rainfalls, there are the dangers of mountain streams becoming raging torrents, and sweeping railway tracks and bridges away bodily. Where railways run along the sea coast, also, there can be the same kind of trouble if the sea piles up under the influence of a gale, and comes rolling up the beaches on a high tide. By far the worst visitation of this kind that Great Britain has ever known occurred at the end of January, 1953; raging waters cut the principal main lines from London to Margate, Tilbury, and Southend, and the Clacton, Harwich and other branches, submerging in all 150 miles of line and marooning innumerable locomotives, coaches and trains. A hurricane of wind blocked many miles of Scottish tracks, and, worst of all, wind and sea sunk the Stranraer-Larne steamer *Princess Victoria*, with the loss of 128 lives.

Washouts through cloudbursts in this country are less frequent, but they are not unknown, by any means. The worst such happening ever known in these islands, probably, was one which attacked Southern Scotland towards the end of August 1948. For many hours the district between Berwick and Dunbar had a storm of wind and sheets of rain that surpassed anything in living memory. There is a little burn called the Eye Water, down whose placid valley there runs the East Coast main line from Edinburgh to Newcastle; it enters this valley at Grantshouse summit, and between there and Berwick crosses and recrosses the stream seven times.

Such a roaring torrent did this stream become that in a few hours, one by one, it swept all these seven bridges away, leaving yawning gaps in the line. When the flood waters had subsided, by some praiseworthy engineering work, temporary bridges had been thrown over the gaps in the track, the mass of soil and rocks that had been swept into the cuttings had been cleared, and the line was open again in no more than a few weeks. Trains had to run over it very slowly until, finally, after nearly two years, the last of the new permanent bridges had been put in position, and full-speed running could be restored.

What can happen to a railway when Nature gets out of hand. In August 1948, a cloudburst over the Berwickshire coast caused a small burn known as the Eye Water to become a raging torrent, sweeping away no fewer than seven bridges between Berwick and Grantshouse summit, on the East Coast main line to Edinburgh. Here is Free Kirk bridge, No. 133, which has lost both arches and abutments, leaving the track suspended over the yawning gap.

For a time this important main line was completely out of action, owing to these washouts, and blockage of the cuttings with rocks and soil. By extremely hard work the track was cleared and the gaps were bridged by temporary wooden structures, the line being reopened several weeks later. Nearly two years elapsed before the last temporary bridge had been replaced by a permanent steel structure, like this Free Kirk bridge, permitting resumption of normal speed.

Railway operation over the Schreiber Division of the Canadian Pacific main line from Montreal to Vancouver, where it skirts the north shore of Lake Superior, is conducted in temperatures that are often well below zero in the depth of winter. Here the lake is frozen as the diesel-electric locomotive pulls its train through Jack Fish tunnel. The tail of the train is seen in the far right background.

In mountainous countries, Nature in her playful moods can be even more devastating. Back in 1934, in the remote vastnesses of the Andes, on the borders of Argentina and Chile, a glacier burst, temporarily damming up a deep mountain gorge. Behind the barrage of ice a great lake built up, until finally the weight of water in its turn burst the ice dam. Then a vast wall of water swept downwards with irresistible force, until it reached the Mendoza valley, in which runs the famous Transandine Railway, on its climb to the summit level of 10,466 feet, at which it cuts through the main chain of the Andes. So many miles of the line, bridges, embankments, track and everything else, were swept away that the railway was closed down completely, and so remained for ten years until the Governments of Chile and Argentina took the derelict line over and completed the tremendous task of reconstruction.

Now, while a burst glacier is a rare event, snow and ice are a problem every winter to railways that have to work in cold climates or high up in the mountains. Light and feathery though the snow is, it has only to fall to a sufficient depth, and it can bring trains to a complete standstill. Or a very strong wind will cause it to drift, and then it may fill up a railway cutting to a much greater depth still. Where drifting is of frequent occurrence, you may see long lines of

175

The highest through railway in Europe — the Bernina section of the Rhaetian Railway, Switzerland, between St. Moritz and Tirano at the Bernina Hospice station, 7,403 ft. above the sea. Trains have been kept working over this line when the snow has been more than 20 ft. deep, running through snow and ice cuttings with vertical sides 15 ft. deep and more. Continuous patrolling with rotary snowploughs is necessary at times when snow is falling.

old railway sleepers stuck up on end alongside the railway, or even more substantial fences, so that the snow may pile up behind them and be prevented from drifting on to the railway; these fences are a common sight, for example, where the Highland main line makes its way through the Grampians by the Druimuachdar pass, north of Blair Atholl, at a height of 1,484 feet above the sea.

But at higher altitudes mere snow fences are not sufficient. Through the bleak highlands of Norway, where the Bergen–Oslo Railway runs for miles at over 4,000 feet altitude, past the Taugevand Lake which even in summer may remain largely frozen over, miles and miles of the line are boxed in completely by continuous timber snowsheds. The same protection may be found on the Canadian Pacific and Canadian National main lines through the Rockies, and on many other high-lying routes.

The avalanche is a more serious problem. Avalanches are usually at their worst when winter is merging into spring, and the warmer winds begin to blow from the south. Then great masses of snow, built up insecurely on steep mountain slopes, break loose and begin to sweep downwards. Like the snowball rolled along the ground, they gather more and more snow as they descend, at ever-increasing speed, and, as they hurl themselves down to lower levels, soil, rocks, uprooted trees, and other solid matter may be caught up into the vast moving mass. At times the speed of the avalanche may reach 100 miles an hour and more, and the hurricane of wind set in motion by its passage may prove as destructive as the avalanche itself.

The dangers are the greatest to railways which are carried high up on precipitous slopes; there is the risk of trains being swept off the lines into the valleys below, or at least completely buried and their occupants suffocated, while electrically-worked lines have the constant menace of their overhead electric equipment being carried away. But so complete are the protection works carried out by the railways that it is extremely rare for a train to suffer disaster through being overwhelmed by an avalanche.

Normally, avalanches follow well-defined tracks. Where a railway crosses one of these danger-spots, the line is covered by an avalanche shelter, massively built

An electrically-operated rotary plough at work on the Bernina line. This is one of the latest type, with twin rotary wheels; in the view both are working counter-clockwise, throwing the snow in a great arc to the left of the track, but either or both can be reversed if necessary.

in reinforced concrete or some similar material. The shelter is made somewhat longer than the greatest probable width of any avalanche sweeping down the track, and has a sharply sloping roof, over which the thundering mass of snow and ice is carried, to drop harmlessly into the valley below.

A whole succession of these avalanche shelters or tunnels can be seen along the Lötschberg Railway in Switzerland, where the line is carried high up on the east wall of the Lonza gorge, on its way from the Lötschberg Tunnel down to the Rhône valley. Not only so, but on the mountainside above the line there innumerable short lengths of masonry wall that have been built to stop and break up the sliding masses of snow before they can reach the railway below and cause an obstruction.

On a neighbouring Swiss line — the narrow-gauge Furka-Oberalp Railway — there is one avalanche protection work that has earned a good deal of fame because of its remarkable ingenuity. Just east of the Furka Tunnel, at a point where the railway is over 6,000 feet above sea level, it crosses the deep and forbidding gorge of the Steffenbach. Down this gorge massive avalanches are of regular occurrence, and the railway authorities have good reason to fear their attentions, for the first bridge thrown over the gorge was swept away in the first winter of its existence.

To make a repetition of this casualty impossible, the engineers of the line have now designed a bridge that takes to pieces, so that it may be stowed away completely during the winter months. This section of the Furka-Oberalp line passes through a part of the Alps that is practically uninhabited in winter, and trains run over it for four summer months of the year only; so the winter interruption of the track by the dismantling of the Steffen-bach bridge does not cause any difficulties.

The bridge is so designed that,

In country where heavy winter snowfall is usual, it is necessary to cover the tracks with shelters of this kind (on the Visp-Zermatt Railway, Switzerland), or with avalanche tunnels, to protect the trains at all points where avalanches may be expected.

with the aid of the derricks which stand at both ends and their wire ropes, dismantling is a relatively simple matter. The diagonal supports which carry the joints between the three spans are hinged both at the top and the bottom; and as the side spans are lifted off the bedstones that carry them and drawn back to rest finally on the track at the two sides of the gorge, so the supporting trestles swing round on their trestles until they lie flat up against the abutment walls of the bridge. The entire width of the gorge is now completely open between the bridge abutments, and the avalanches can sweep through without causing the railway authorities the slightest concern.

So efficient is the work of dismantling and re-erection that

Winter conditions make the operation of the Norwegian Bergen-Oslo Railway extremely difficult. Note the timber extension of the Reinunga tunnel, to prevent blockage of the entrance by snowdrifts, and also the snow fence in the foreground, designed to prevent drifting as far as possible. At times the Taugevand lake, skirted by this railway at over 4,200 ft. altitude and bordered with glaciers, remains frozen throughout the summer as well as the winter.

The ingenious Steffenbach bridge, on the Swiss Furka-Oberalp Railway. This line is closed throughout the winter, and as the gorge is subject to destructive avalanches, the bridge is designed to be taken to pieces every late autumn and stowed away on both sides of the gorge. The side spans are lifted clear and drawn back till they rest on the track, the diagonal struts swinging round on hinges to come to rest against the abutment walls.

each operation now can be completed in a single day.

It is impossible, of course, to cover the whole of any line of railway that may become blocked by exceptional snowfall, and all railways running through areas in which snow may fall heavily in wintertime must be provided with means for clearing their lines quickly. In the North of England the usual method is to fit the engine with a contrivance which looks like a pair of butterfly wings, beneath the buffers; this form of plough shoulders the snow to right and left as the engine moves forward, but cannot deal with more than three feet or so of snow. With any greater depth than this there must be the more laborious task of shifting the snow by hand with shovels, which may take a very considerable time, and still leaves the snow sufficiently near the line to drift back if there is a strong wind.

Railways that are troubled with severe snow conditions every winter, such as those in Switzerland, have much more efficient snow-clearing equipment. This is in the form of the rotary snow-plough. Mounted on these ploughs, at the 'business' end, is the rotary, a wheel extending to the full width of the vehicle, and with vanes mounted on its spokes from the centre to the circumference. Inside the casing behind the rotary there is a boiler and an engine used to spin the rotary round.

On Western Region main lines immediately in advance of every 'distant' signal, ramps are laid down between the running rails of the track. Below each locomotive (left-hand view) is a shoe which comes into contact with the ramp. When the signal is in the 'clear' position, an electric current passes through the ramp, and is picked up by the shoe; this causes the bell to ring in the engine-cab (right-hand view) between the two windows. When the signal is in the horizontal or 'caution' position, the ramp is dead; contact with the engine shoe then sounds a loud horn in the cab, instead of the bell, and automatically makes a brake application. This is of the greatest assistance to a driver in foggy weather, for it enables him to 'hear' a signal that he may not be able to see.

Pushed by one or more locomotives, the plough advances into the snowdrift, with the wheel rotating; the vanes are so shaped as to cut through the snow and to throw it upwards through the casing and in a wide arc to fifty feet or more clear of the track. According to the direction of rotation, so the snow is thrown to left or right of the track at will. The latest Swiss snow-ploughs have twin rotaries of rather smaller diameter, throwing the snow to left and right simultaneously, and these are even more efficient. On a Swiss line like the Bernina, which goes over 7,400 feet altitude in the Bernina Pass, with the help of the rotary plough traffic has been kept going when the snow has been over twenty feet deep.

Another enemy of the railways is frost. Its most severe effects are felt when rain falls after a severe frost, and freezes over everything on which it deposits itself. The worst sufferers here are electric railways on which the trains or locomotives pick up their current from a third rail, for a coating of ice on this rail acts as a non-conductor, and can bring the electric trains to a complete standstill. At night you have only to use your eyes to realize that this is happening, for the brilliant flashes, or 'arcing', as the collecting shoes of the electric motors try to make contact with the rail, can be seen for miles around. Special 'de-icing' trains have to be run, when this particular type of weather threatens, in an endeavour to keep the conductor rails ice-free.

In similar weather conditions, ice will build up on wires also, and if a gale should spring up at the same time, the strain on telegraph and other wires, owing to the tremendous additional weight that they are being forced to carry, becomes so great that the wires, or the poles supporting them, can stand it no longer. Sometimes miles and miles of wire have been blown down in this way, causing chaos in railway operation because all the signalling circuits get broken, and it is impossible for each signal box to communicate with the next.

At the beginning of this chapter we thought of fog, which produces dangers of another kind because it reduces visibility, so that drivers cannot see their signals. If fog is coming on, as soon as certain signals can no longer be seen from the signalbox, the signalman must call out the 'fogmen'. Usually these are the men responsible for working on the track; and as the fog prevents them from carrying on their work in safety, they are used instead for fog signalling.

Automatic train control, or 'a.t.c.', is standard equipment on all American high-speed main lines; the indications of the lineside signals are repeated on a panel inside the driver's cab, and brakes are applied automatically if the signal aspects are adverse. On the Pennsylvania R.R. main line from New York to Washington, the signalling is by white lights on the circular disc seen through the cab window of this electric locomotive; three vertical lights mean 'clear', and they are repeated in the uppermost of the five openings in the vertical signal panel on the left of the cab.

All 'key' signals are manned in this way. It is the business of the fogman to keep a detonator on the rail all the time that his particular signal is at danger or caution, and to take it off as soon as the signal is pulled to 'clear'. This method of warning drivers by an explosion under their engines is a very primitive one, and in a thick fog the traffic can be slowed down to a terrible degree while the drivers are crawling from one signal, at which they have been checked, to the next, which may also be at danger.

Many years ago the Great Western Railway, as it then was, devised a system of 'automatic train control' specially to speed up the trains and to ensure safer working in fog, and by degrees equipped all their main lines with it, as described already in Chapter 13. In thick weather, the Western Region driver can carry on quite safely at speed while he hears a succession of bell rings, but the moment the ring is exchanged for the blast of the horn, slowing down is essential. While this apparatus is not a perfect protection, the Western Region is able to work its trains a good deal faster in foggy weather than any other Region of British Railways, and also has the best record of any part of the railways of this country for freedom from collisions. An automatic train control apparatus of another kind is installed on the Eastern Region line between Fenchurch Street and Southend-on-Sea, and another is under trial on the Eastern Region main line out of King's Cross.

So the railways, in these and many other ways, have constantly to keep a wary eye on Nature and her little tricks, which add in no small degree to the cost of equipping and operating the lines. In view of all the things that can happen in bad weather, it is amazing how seldom traffic is interrupted in this way, and how quickly the railways succeed in restoring their communications.

One of the worst storm disasters in British railway history was the blowing down of the central portion of the Tay Bridge in a furious gale one night in December 1879. The night mail, crossing at the time, was engulfed in the waters, and all on board were drowned. The stumps of the piers of the original bridge, in the design of which insufficient allowance had been made for extreme wind pressure, can be seen to the right of the present bridge. The Tay Bridge, 11,653 ft. long, holds the record for length in Great Britain.

CHAPTER 16

Seen by the lineside

THERE is a fascination about the steam locomotive. No other form of transport is really able to rival it. To most of us the aeroplane is little more than a dot in the sky, and it is seldom that we see anything of an aeroplane at close quarters. Similarly with the giants of the sea; we may see them from time to time when we are by the seaside on holiday, but usually at a considerable distance away. The locomotive, however, is something close at hand; we can see its machinery in motion and grasp at a glance something of the way in which it works; from the station platform we can see the driver and fireman in the cab, and note the way in which they handle their controls; we can travel behind it and enjoy all the sensations of speed as the countryside flashes by.

It might be said that the same applies to the motor car or the motor-coach; but somehow the steam locomotive leaves all these rivals behind in interest. Equally on the railway itself, it is never possible to be stirred to quite the same degree at the sight of an electric train, no matter how fast it may be travelling, or by one of the newest diesel-electric or gas-turbine-electric locomotives purring along. They look so very much alike; and they have not the distinctive voice of the steam locomotive as it sets about its work, blasting up some steep gradient or pulsating contentedly along over a flatter stretch of line, and leaving behind it a long trail of feathery white exhaust steam. No; the steam locomotive behaves like a living creature, working, talking, sometimes shouting, at other times wheezing because it needs the attention of the doctor — a thing of life.

Part of the interest, of course, lies in unending variety. Unfortunately this variety is diminishing, and will continue to diminish, with nationalization. Up to the end of 1922 there were a large number of different railways in Great Britain, each with its own locomotive designs and its own distinctive colours. Then, as described at the end of Chapter 1, there came the grouping that reduced all this variety to four main line railways only, and each of these railways soon set about reducing the vast numbers of its different locomotive types to as few standard classes as possible, in order to economize in maintenance. Now, with nationalization, we have one railway system only, and a few British Railways standard classes are being introduced which eventually will supersede all the many varieties of locomotive which still exist in Great Britain. Happily, however, a great deal of the old variety may still be seen in active service, and will remain so for a good many years to come.

Now, one outcome of the steam locomotive's fascination has been the tremendous interest that it has aroused among boys in the art of 'spotting'. I have no doubt that many of you who will read this book are numbered among those who neglect no opportunity of getting

A typical British lineside view. The southbound 'Flying Scotsman' is passing Shaftholme Junction; from the opening of the East Coast main line in 1850 trains passed here from Great Northern on to North Eastern metals. To the left is the Knottingley branch, which belonged to the Lancashire & Yorkshire Railway. Notice to the right of the signalbox the figure '20', with an arrow pointing left, showing that the speed on taking the branch should not exceed 20 m.p.h. Notice also the two white headlamps carried at each end of the engine buffer-beam, indicating a Class 'A', or 'Express Passenger' train.

to the lineside, with their notebooks, in order to record the numbers of all the locomotives that pass their point of vantage. If this applies to you, then this chapter is being written for your special benefit. For the intelligent 'spotter' is not one who is merely content to jot down a series of numbers of engines that he has seen. A sharp eye can note a great many details about a locomotive that are of interest, and if these are entered in the record also, they will add very greatly to the pleasure and the instruction to be obtained from 'spotting'.

Apart from the number itself, the first point to be noted about a locomotive is its wheel arrangement, which largely helps to decide the type of work for which it is intended. In Chapter 4 we dealt with the notation by which the arrangement of wheels is described in figures — 4–6–2 for the big Pacifics, for example, 4–6–0 for engines like the Western Region 'Kings' and 'Castles' or the London Midland Region 'Royal Scots', and so on. The three names just mentioned are a reminder, also, that locomotives are divided up into classes, each one of which represents a different design, and here the 'spotter' can find endless entertainment in deciding, from what he sees of it in the distance, the particular class of engine that is approaching him.

On the Western Region the classes are indicated largely by the names the engines bear — 'Kings', 'Castles', 'Stars', 'Saints', 'Counties', 'Halls', 'Manors' and 'Granges' — but these apply

184

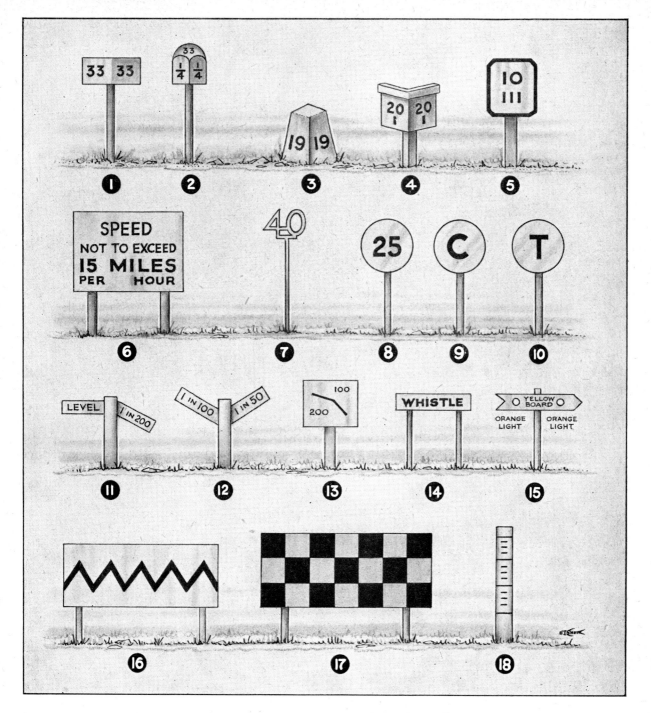

LINESIDE INDICATIONS

1. Mile post (33 miles). Midland Division, London Midland Region.
2. Mile post (33¼ miles). Midland Division, London Midland Region.
3 & 4. Concrete mile posts. (19 miles and 20¼ miles).
5. Metal plate mile post (10¾ miles). (There are also a number of other varieties of mile posts).
6, 7 & 8. Maximum speed limit signs (miles per hour). Number 7 on Eastern and North Eastern Regions only.
9. Temporary speed restriction commences.
10. Temporary speed restriction terminates.
11, 12 & 13. Types of gradient posts.
14. Whistle order board.
15. Distant warning of temporary speed restriction.
16. Water trough warning board. Eastern Region only.
17. Postal apparatus warning board. Black and yellow checker board.
18. Levelling post. Used where subsidence trouble is experienced.

A typical American lineside view. For the most part, American railways are not fenced in, and it is therefore compulsory by law to fit every American locomotive with a powerful headlamp, illuminating the track for a long distance ahead; with a 'cow-catcher', or steel fender, to deal with cattle or other obstructions which may get on to the line; and with a bell, seen above the smokebox, to give warning in towns where railway tracks may run along the streets. This huge 4–6–6–4 articulated locomotive, with 14-wheel tender, on the Union Pacific main line in Echo Canyon, Utah.

only to engines which take at least some share in passenger working. On the London Midland Region, classification is not so easy, because the many different types of engine are grouped together into eight 'power' classes only, so that Class '5MT', for example, merely indicates that the engine concerned is in Power Class '5' and is suitable for 'Mixed Traffic' — that is, either passenger or freight trains. The use of the 'T' in this connection is confusing, as the suffix 'T' is also in general use to signify a 'tank' engine, which, as you remember, is the type of locomotive for short distance work that carries its supplies of coal and water on its own main frames, and needs no separate tender. Thus a '2–6–4 T' is the designation of a 2–6–4 tank engine. This suffix is sometimes expanded to 'ST', for 'saddle tank', or 'PT' for 'pannier tank', if the water supply is carried above the boiler, as described in Chapter 4.

Class designations on the Eastern and North Eastern Regions follow those of the late London & North Eastern Railway, and go into far more detail. Each consists of a number and a letter; the letter indicates the wheel arrangement and the number the precise class of engine in that wheel arrangement. Every 'A' locomotive, for example, is a 4–6–2; the last Pacific tender engines built to London & North Eastern Railway designs are in Class 'A1', but by far the most famous class is Gresley's streamlined 'A4', which includes *Mallard* and most of the other engines that made the principal speed records in London & North Eastern Railway days. 'B' is the group letter for 4–6–0 engines, 'J' for 0–6–0 engines, and so on. Engine classes on the Southern Region are also indicated by letters and numbers, but not so clearly and distinctively divided up as those of the late London & North Eastern Railway.

As most 'spotters' know, there are inexpensive booklets available which give complete lists of the locomotive numbers of all British Railways locomotives, with the class to which each locomotive belongs, and other details of great interest, such as the former railways with which various locomotive types originated, the dates when the first examples were built, and the leading dimensions of each class. A study of these details, compared with what you see at the lineside, will give you a really thorough knowledge of the locomotives of this country. An even more fascinating line of study is to note particular ways in which individual engines have been altered in such a way that in some detail or other they differ from the remaining engines of the class. Experiments of this kind are often made, and it will train your powers of observation to note down any such peculiarities as the engines pass.

Another point to note about a locomotive is where it lives when it is at home. Chapter 5 has explained that every locomotive is attached to a depot, or 'shed', for purposes of main-tenance. If it is making a lengthy continuous run, so that return to the home shed is impossible in the same twenty-four hours, it may 'board out' at the shed at the further end of its journey, and return home the following day. Sometimes, in order that the maximum use may be made of the services of a locomotive, and especially one of a 'mixed traffic' type, it may make a circular tour which will take it away from its home shed for several days.

Modern British engines now show where they are normally located; on the upper part of the smokebox door is seen the locomotive's number, and on the lower part of the door, on a small circular plate, there may be seen a number and a letter. The number is that of the dis-

In the early days of railways, it was necessary for all the cuttings, of no matter what depth (as, for example, Tring cutting, illustrated on page 17) to be cut out laboriously by an enormous number of navvies, armed with spades and barrows; the soil might then have to be wheeled for considerable distances to where it was needed for making an embankment. Today powerful earth-moving machinery, like that illustrated here making a new line for the Union Pacific R.R., cuts the labour force and the time to completion down to a mere fraction of what were needed previously.

Much has been done in recent years to 'tidy up' railway property and improve its appearance. The North Eastern Region of British Railways has been particularly active in this respect, and this view, at Northallerton, is a striking example of what can be done. A waste piece of land between two sets of tracks now is occupied by lawns with shrubs and neat concrete edgings, bordered by paths of broken grey stone.

trict to which the locomotive belongs, and the latter indicates the actual shed to which it is attached. As typical examples there may be mentioned '1B' on the London Midland Region, '1' for Willesden District and 'B' for Camden shed; '9A' for Manchester Longsight; '34A' for London King's Cross, Eastern Region; '52A' for Gateshead, North Eastern Region; '70A' for Nine Elms, Southern Region; '81A' for Old Oak Common, the principal London shed of the Western Region; and so on.

The booklets of locomotive numbers which I have mentioned usually contain a list of the shed numbers, and so are very helpful in shed 'spotting'. It is a most intriguing business to note, from the shed number carried by a locomotive, where it has come from, and every now and again to 'spot' a complete stranger that by some means or other has come down, say, all the way from the North of Scotland to the London area.

It only remains to be added that the serious 'spotter' makes his lineside notes in a rough notebook, or on loose sheets of paper, and keeps at home the proper notebook in which all his notes are entered. This should be a book of reasonable size, ruled into columns in such a way as to permit entering the engine number, wheel arrangement, class and power class (if known), and shed, with a space at the right-hand side in which to note any special feature or peculiarity of an individual engine. This will make your 'spotting' a really informative occupation.

I have never heard of anyone setting out to 'spot' coaches, although there is a great deal of interest in noting how trains are composed, and especially so in these days of shortage of

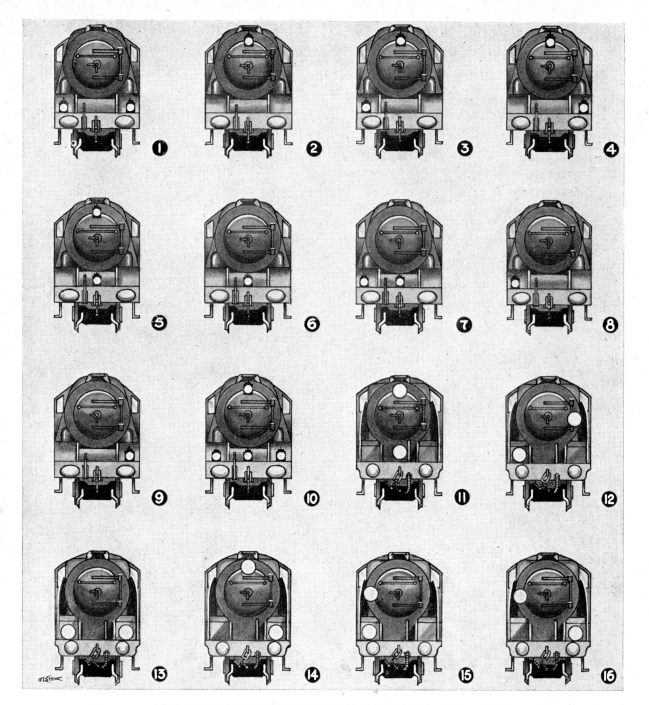

BRITISH RAILWAYS ENGINE HEADLIGHTS AND DISCS

1. Express passenger, newspaper, or breakdown train or express diesel car, Class 'A'.
2. Ordinary passenger, branch passenger, or 'mixed' train, or diesel or other rail-motor, Class 'B'.
3. Express freight, livestock, or 'perishable' train with not less than one-third of the wagons continuously braked and piped to the engine, Class 'D'.
4. Express freight, livestock, or ballast train not fitted with the continuous brake, Class 'F'.
5. Through freight train or mineral train not fitted with the continuous brake, Class 'H'.
6. Light engine or engines, or engine with not more than two brake vans attached, Class 'G'.
7. Empty coach, parcels, livestock, 'perishable', or milk train composed of coaching stock; express freight train

piped throughout and with continuous brakes operating on at least half the vehicles, Class 'C'.
8. Mineral or empty wagon train, Class 'J'.
9. Pick-up or branch freight, mineral or ballast train, Class 'K'.
10. Royal train.
11. Southern Region, Waterloo-Salisbury-Exeter-Plymouth.
12. Southern Region, Waterloo-Southampton-Bournemouth.
13. Southern Region, Victoria-Dover, *via* Tonbridge and Ashford, Cannon Street-Ramsgate, *via* Chatham.
14. S.R., Victoria-Ramsgate, *via* Chatham and Margate.
15. S.R., Victoria-Newhaven Harbour boat trains.
16. S.R., Holborn Viaduct-Chatham-Margate-Ramsgate.

Note: On the Southern Region the lamps are replaced in daytime by white discs.

189

rolling stock. For at such times as summer week-ends, when every available vehicle has to be pressed into service in order to cope with the traffic, all kinds of extraordinary mixtures of stock may be seen in the trains by those who are keen-sighted enough to recognize the origin of some of the veteran coaches.

In earlier days, there were very considerable differences in coach design between the outlines of the vehicles built by different companies, and many of the old coaches have survived considerably longer than the old locomotives. Sometimes in a single train you can see half-a-dozen varieties of coaches, and more, that have drifted to one area from all parts of England and Scotland. Unfortunately I have not space in which to develop this side of the subject. For myself, recognition is easy, as I lived for years in the days of the old original companies, but to those of you who are younger, recognition is only possible, probably,

Prominent lineside object at any of the larger locomotive depots is the coaling plant. This plant, at Whitemoor, Cambridgeshire, includes a hydraulic hoist which lifts the coal wagon bodily to the top of the tower. Here the wagon, firmly gripped, is turned over, so that its contents fall into the capacious bunker inside the tower. Locomotives pass under the tower one by one; by electric controls the lower doors of the bunker are opened, and the exact quantity of coal required is weighed automatically and dropped on to the tender. A minute or two suffices to complete the operation, as compared with the laborious hand coaling of earlier days.

if you are able to consult the railway periodicals of this earlier period, in which the various types of vehicle were illustrated.

Still another point of interest at the lineside is to check how the trains are running; this means taking a timetable with you and recognizing each passenger train as it passes. Very informative records can be compiled in this way; as to whether each train is on time, or how many minutes it is early or late; of the type of engine that hauls it and the shed from which it comes (and by noting the number of the engine you may be able to trace, later on in the day, the normal return working of the same engine); and how many coaches are being hauled. You may be excited at times to notice that an unusual type of engine is working some particular express; the regular engine may have failed, and an engine of a lower power class may have succeeded in keeping time with the train. Or you may see how an exceptionally heavy load has caused time to be lost. There is endless entertainment to be obtained from intelligent lineside 'spotting'.

Equally, when you travel in the train, there are many things of interest at the lineside to be seen from the railway carriage window. A page in this chapter has been devoted to some of the many varieties of indications that are installed by the side of the line, to serve different purposes. For example, there are the distance posts, with which every line of railway is marked out at quarter-mile intervals. These are of many different forms, because all the original railways had their own types of post, and neither grouping nor nationalization have caused these to be altered. On some lines, like the London Midland main line out of Euston or the Eastern main line out of King's Cross, the 'mile-posts', as they are generally known, are on the left-hand side of the track, as one looks along the train towards the engine; on others, like the Western main line out of Paddington or the Midland out of St. Pancras, they are on the right.

One valuable use of mileposts to the traveller is that they enable him to take records of train speeds by timing from post to post. For really accurate work, a stop-watch is necessary; if times are read from the second-hand of an ordinary watch, they should not be taken over shorter distances than half-a-mile or a mile, but with a stop-watch reading to one-fifth of a second, quarter-mile records may be relied on. In 'clocking' between mile-posts, the observer should keep his eye on some fixed line in his coach, like that of a window-frame, hold his head steady, and catch the post just as it 'hits' his line; otherwise his readings may be too approximate for accuracy.

Incidentally, there is another method of recording for those with sharp hearing. It is to time off the rail-joints as the train passes over them. Rails are cut very accurately to length; 60 feet is the general standard in this country, so that 22 such rails make a quarter-of-a-mile. The recorder should therefore count up to 22 beats from the joints, starting his count and his stop-watch at zero, and stopping it on the 22nd beat, which is the end of $\frac{1}{4}$-mile, by which he obtains the exact time over that distance. The equivalent speeds for the various times recorded are easily worked out, and should be carried in tabular form in the pocket or in the notebook.

Careful train timing is a most interesting occupation for a journey. It involves noting the starting time, the time of passing all the stations *en route*, and the time of coming to a dead stand, also the highest and lowest speeds on the down gradients and up gradients respectively. If accurate records are desired, starting, stopping and passing times should be read to both minutes and seconds, but this can be done with any good wrist- or pocket-watch. Train timing really requires a knowledge of the route over which one is travelling, and its gradients, but again there are various books that provide the keen train-timer with 'gradient profiles' of the principal main lines. These give him a good idea where high and low speeds may be expected, and show him where it is desirable to take passing times at such locations as summits, where there is no station; in such cases the time must be read to a signalbox or milepost.

Actually, the timing of trains is a highly specialized art. To those who practise it, it can at times prove most exciting, especially on the day of days when one finds all one's previous records of times and speeds on some train or route going by the board as a particularly brilliant piece of work is being done by the locomotive. Yes, here again the steam locomotive appeals as being a living creature, and the study of the 'form' of the iron horse can be just as absorbing as that of his flesh-and-blood brother on the race track. So, whether you become a lineside 'spotter', a train timer, or in whatever way the railway interest may throw its hold over you, my best wish to you is 'Good hunting!'

The tail of the 'Queen of Scots', one of Britain's luxury all-Pullman trains, setting out on its long journey from King's Cross to Glasgow by way of Leeds, Harrogate, Newcastle and Edinburgh, a total of just over 451 miles.